Angel Romero – Bella

Music transcriptions by Angel Romero

ISBN 978-1-4234-6823-3

HAL•LEONARD®
CORPORATION
7777 W. BLUEMOUND RD. P.O. BOX 13819 MILWAUKEE, WI 53213

For all works contained herein:
Unauthorized copying, arranging, adapting, recording, Internet posting, public performance,
or other distribution of the printed music in this publication is an infringement of copyright.
Infringers are liable under the law.

Visit Hal Leonard Online at
www.halleonard.com

Dedication

For many years I have devoted my life to making people happy with my music, yet somehow I've neglected to publish my arrangements. Since I was a child, I have loved music with all my heart—not only the works written for my beloved instrument, the guitar, but also symphonic music. As a young man, this led me to study conducting, which has enabled me to interpret the great works of Beethoven, Brahms, Mahler, Mozart, and many other great composers. Nonetheless, I have always been aware that my instrument is a small orchestra in itself. The guitar with its intimate voice can reach our soul to the maximum.

When I was asked to make a recording with some of the great classics, I decided to be brave and a bit crazy. I chose to play some of the great works for piano and other instruments that were very close to my heart, always facing the danger of being criticized negatively for my ambitious attempt.

A few months before my recording, my wife Nefretiri and I had a beautiful little girl born on January 12, 2001. We named her Isabella, but we always called her Bella, which literally means "beautiful." When I would sit down to work on the recording, I would play the music and she would smile at me. During all the recording sessions, my wife would bring her to the studio and this made Bella very happy. When the recording was finished, the producers were trying to find a name for the record. Without hesitation they all looked at each other and said, "Let's name it 'Bella' since the repertoire in this record is beautiful music, and your daughter smiled all the time you were recording."

I dedicate these transcriptions to the great inspirations of the composers and, of course, to my little muse, my daughter Bella.

Angel Romero
May, 2011

La Paloma

By Sebastian de Yradier
Transcribed by Francisco Tarrega
Arranged by Angel Romero

Tuning:
(low to high) D-A-D-G-B-E

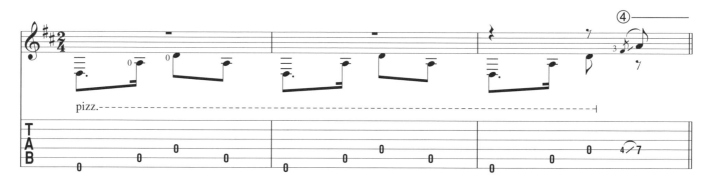

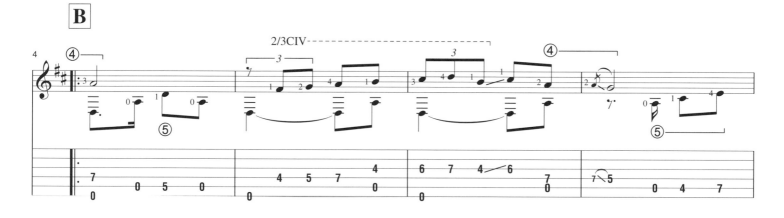

*Harmonics sound *8va* throughout.

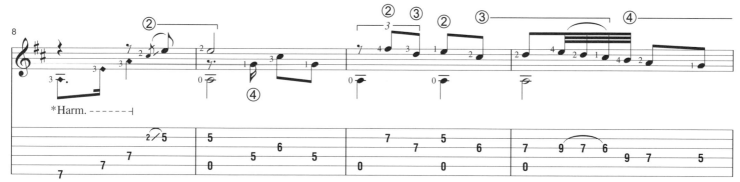

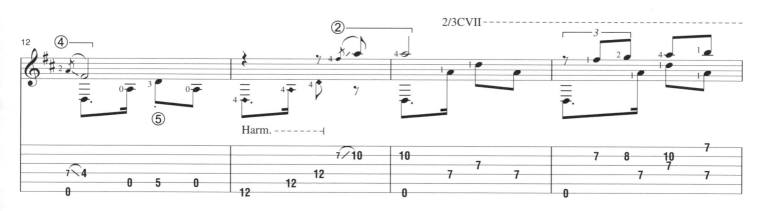

Copyright © 2010 by Angel Romero
All Rights Reserved   Used by Permission

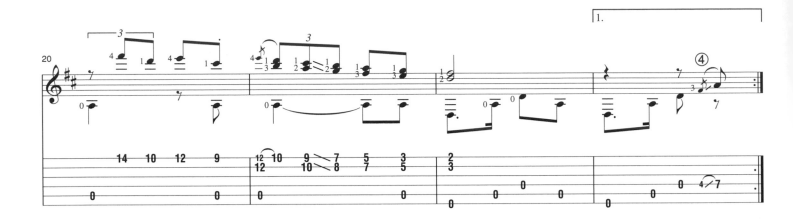

*2nd time, pizz.

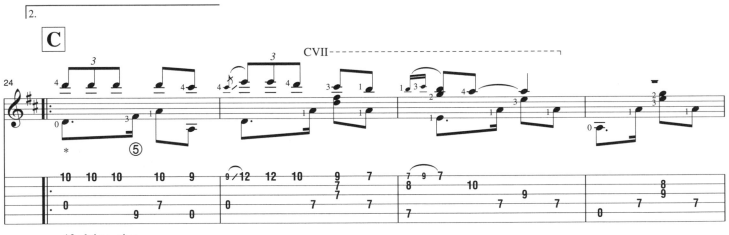

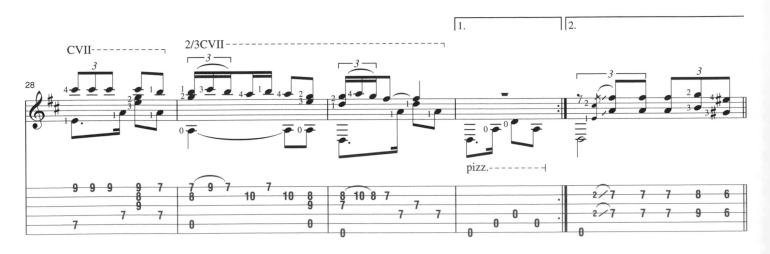

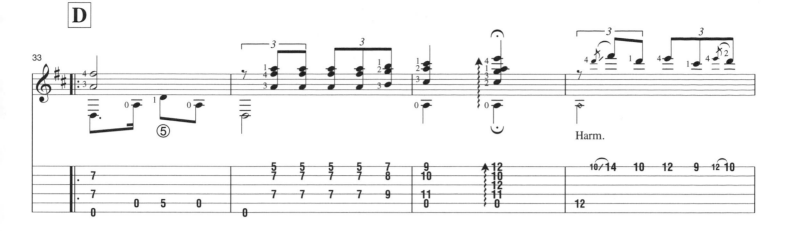

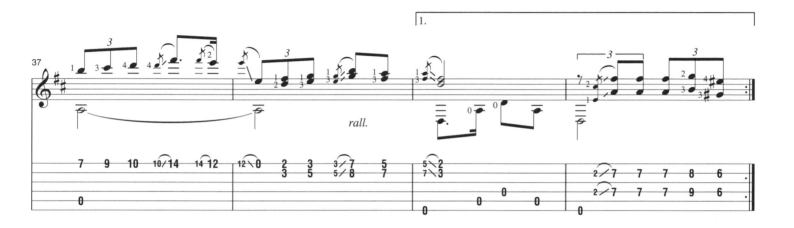

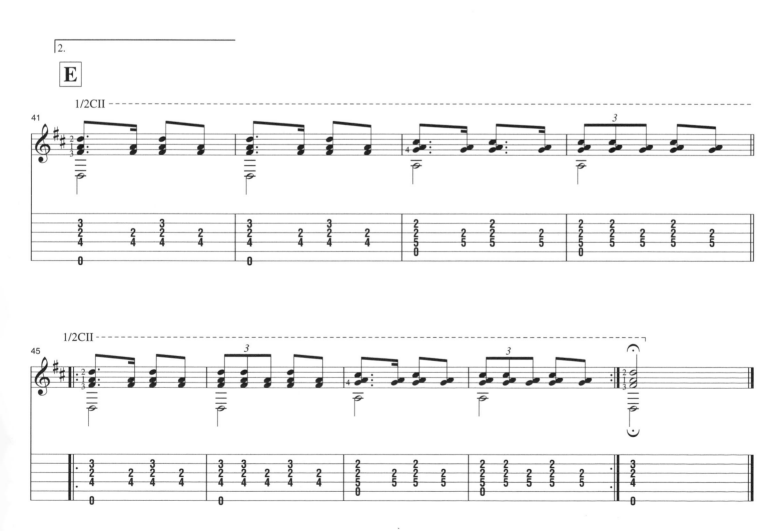

Meditation
from Thais

By Jules Massenet
Arranged and Transcribed for guitar by Angel Romero

Tuning:
(low to high) D-A-D-G-B-E

Andante

very legato

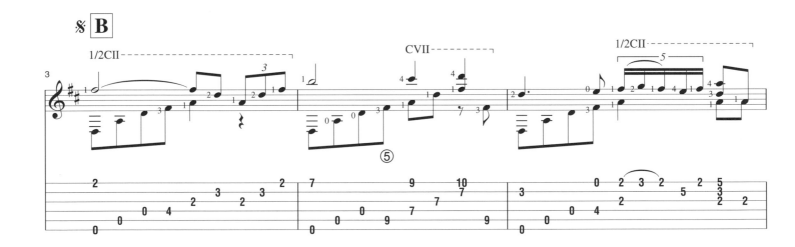

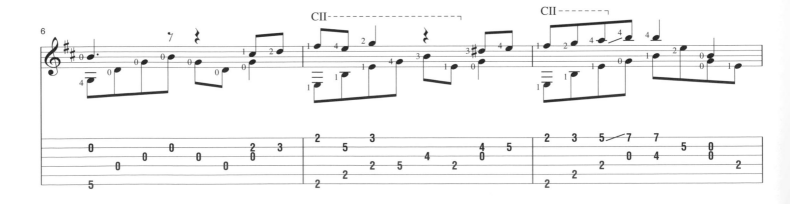

Copyright © 2001 by Angel Romero
All Rights Reserved   Used by Permission

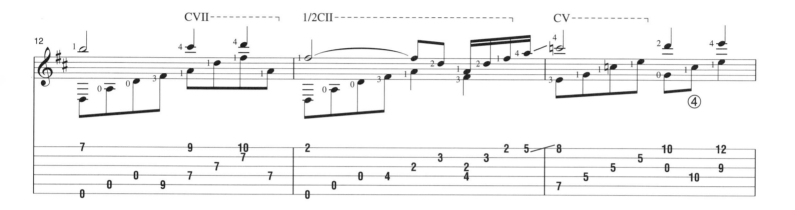

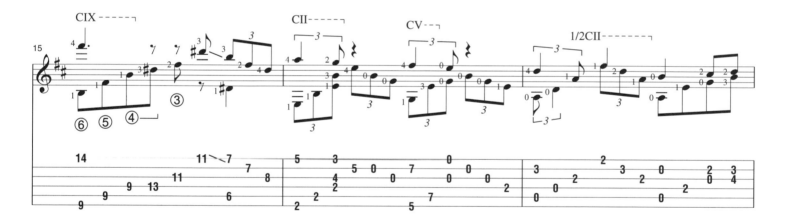

C

A tempo

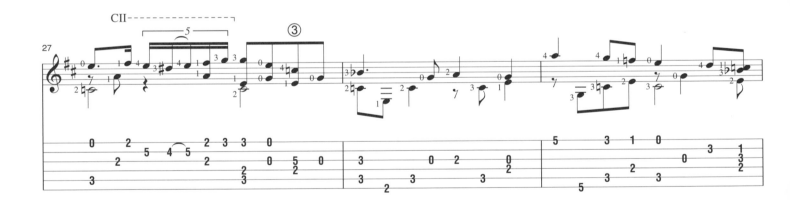

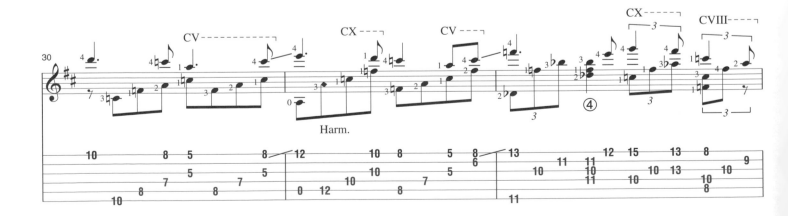

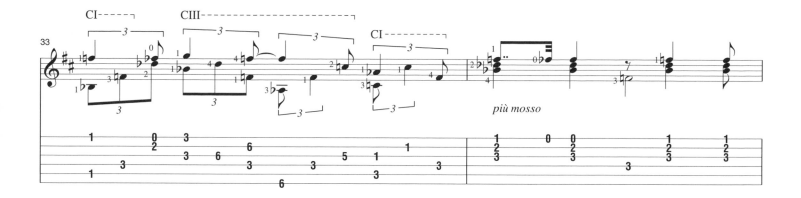

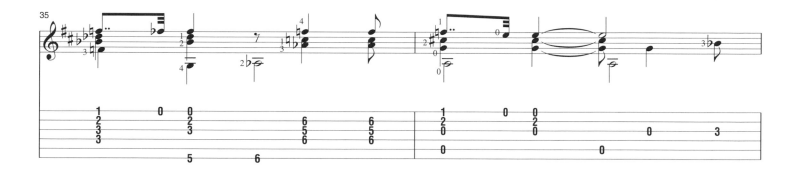

D.S. al Coda

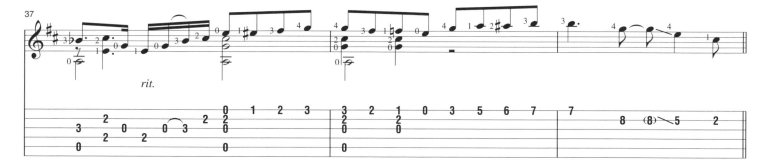

⊕ **Coda**

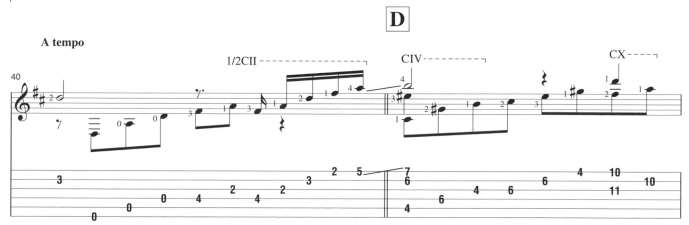

A tempo

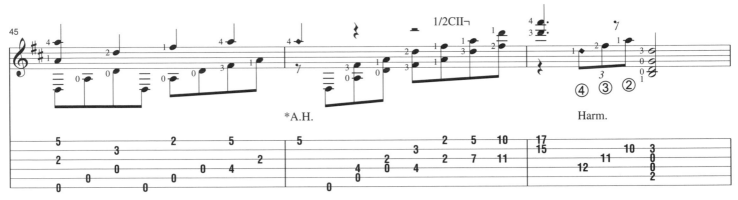

*Artificial harmonics sound *8va* throughout.

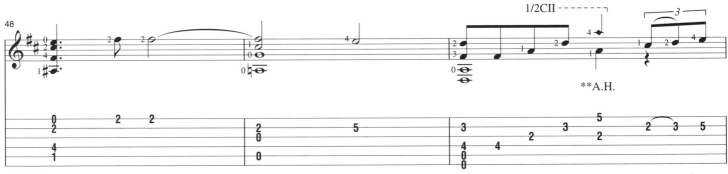

**1st string only, next 2 meas.

Somewhere in Time
from *Somewhere in Time*

By John Barry

Tuning:
(low to high) D-A-D-G-B-E

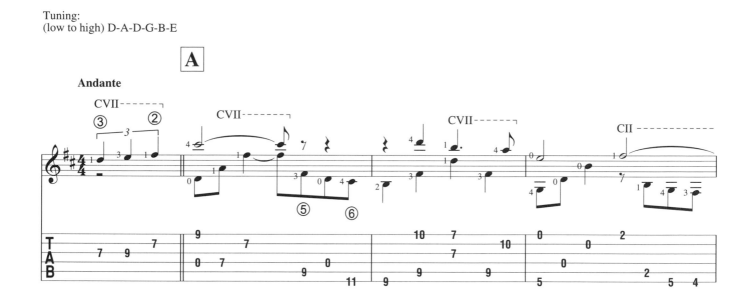

Copyright © 1980 USI B GLOBAL MUSIC PUBLISHING and HIT & RUN MUSIC LTD.
All Rights Controlled and Administered by SONGS OF UNIVERSAL, INC.
All Rights Reserved   Used by Permission

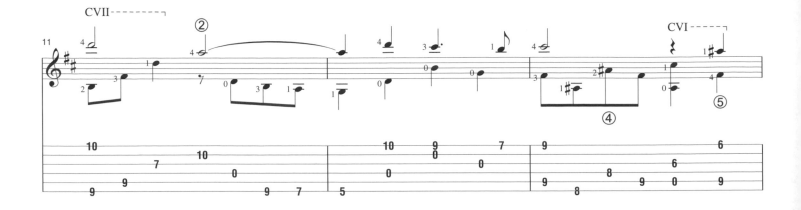

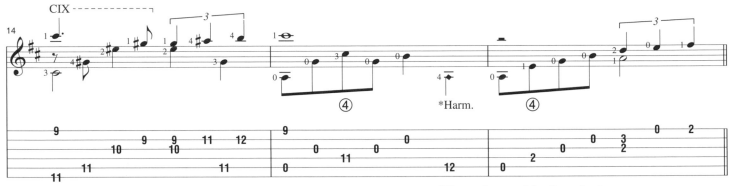

*Harmonics sound *8va* throughout.

B

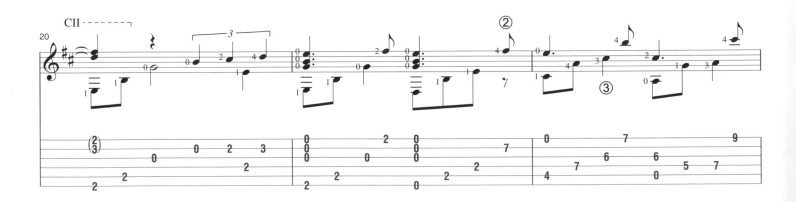

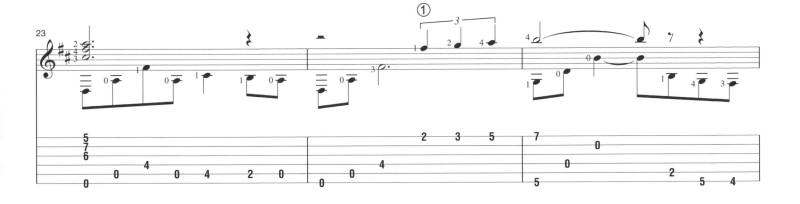

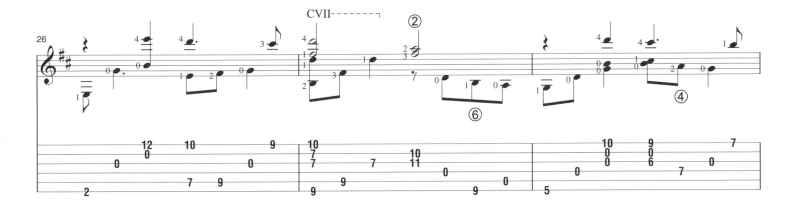

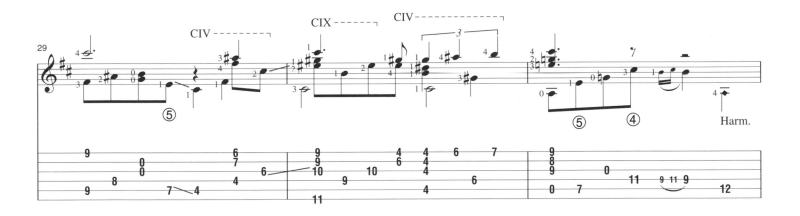

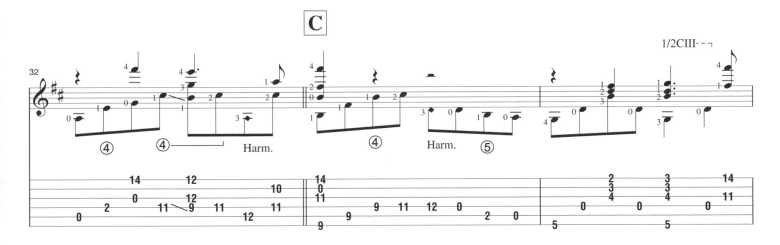

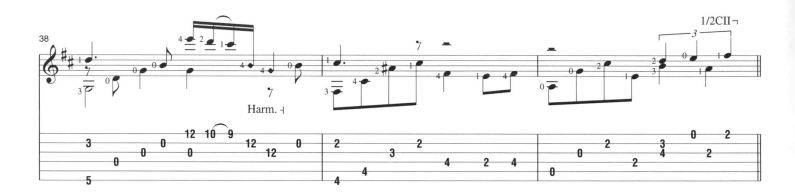

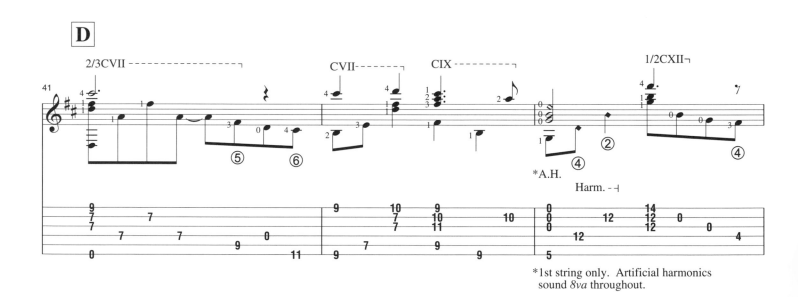

D

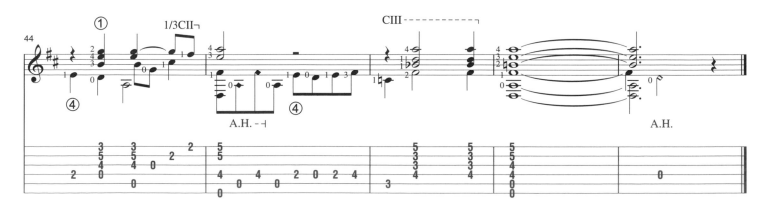

*1st string only. Artificial harmonics
sound *8va* throughout.

Tango Angelita

Words and Music by Celedonio Romero
Arranged by Angel Romero

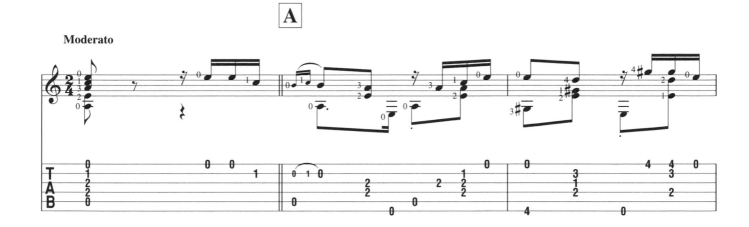

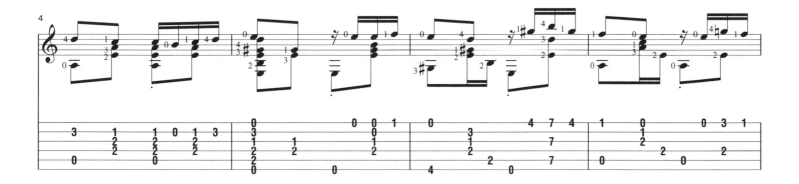

Copyright © 2010 by Angel Romero
All Rights Reserved   Used by Permission

17

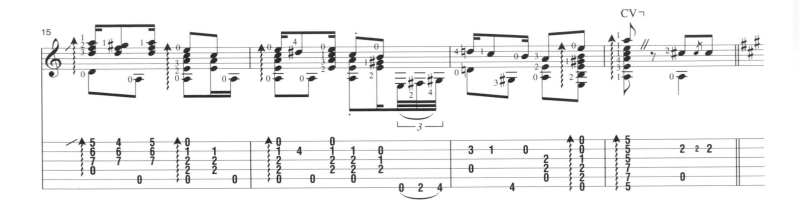

B

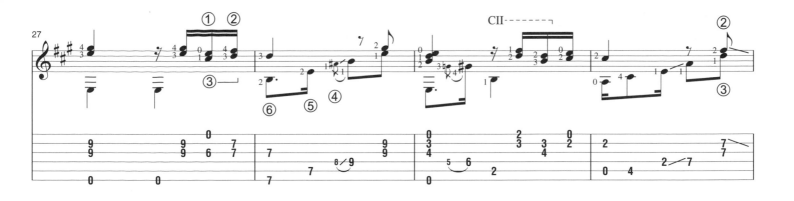

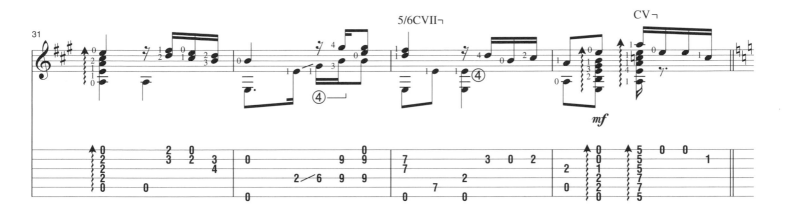

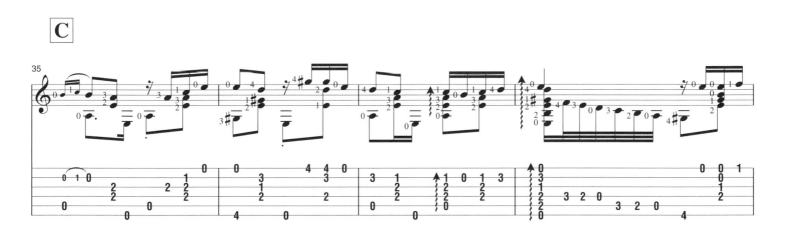

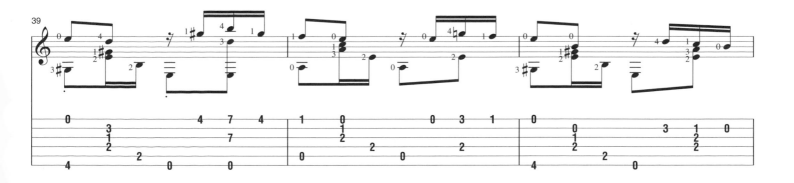

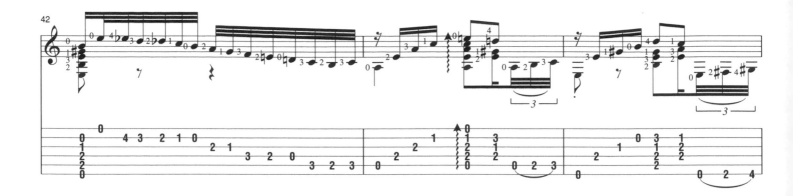

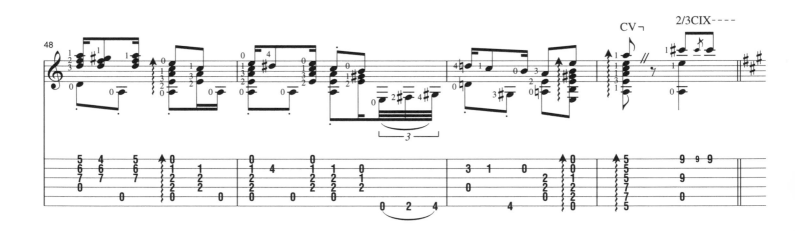

D

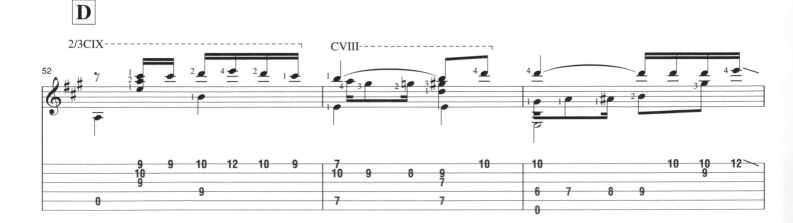

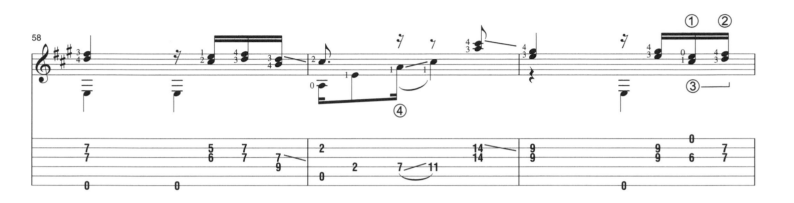

La fille aux cheveux de lin
(The Girl with the Flaxen Hair)

By Claude Debussy
Arranged by Angel Romero

A

Très calme et doucement expressif ♩ = 66

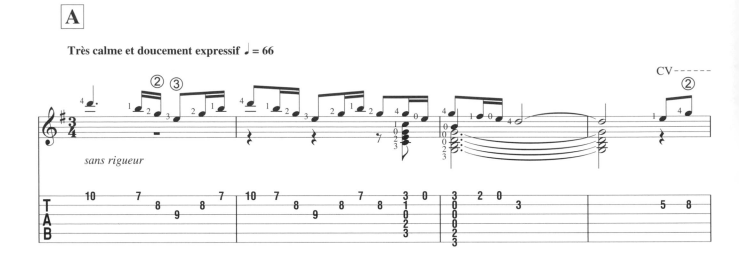

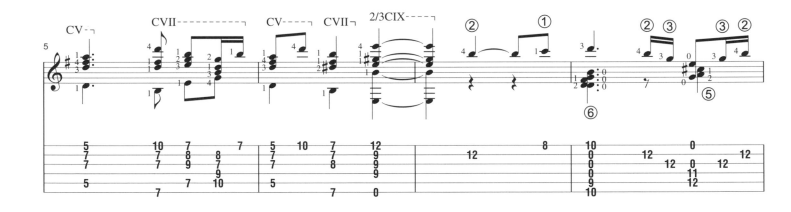

Copyright © 2010 by Angel Romero
All Rights Reserved   Used by Permission

Mouv!

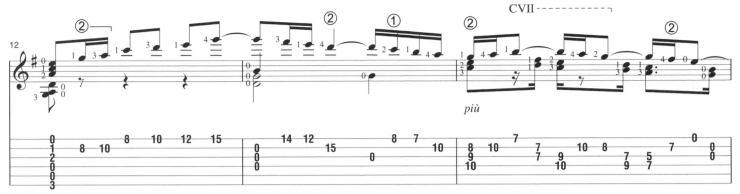

più

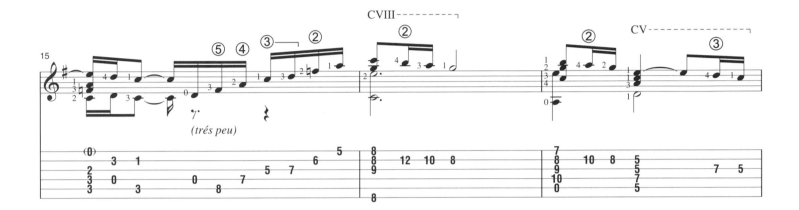

(trés peu)

B

Un peu animé

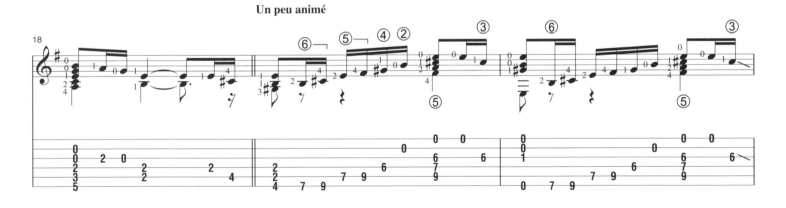

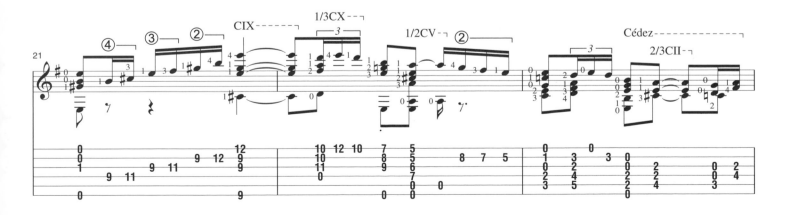

Mouv! *(sans lourdeur)*

Cédez------------┐

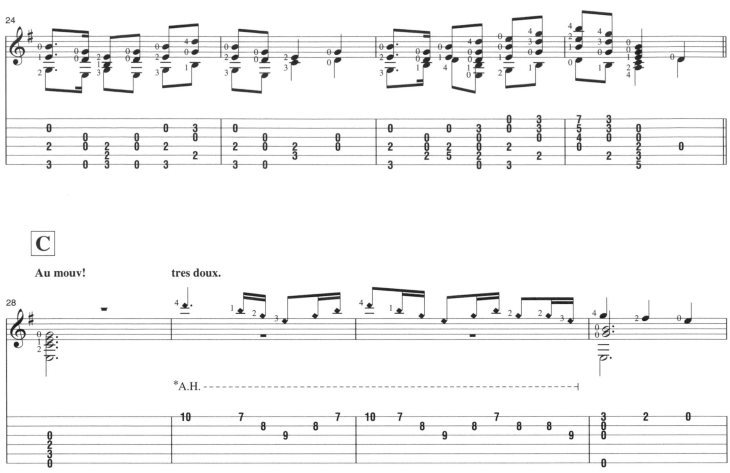

C

Au mouv!   **tres doux.**

*A.H.--

*Artificial harmonics sound *8va* throughout.

Murmuré et en retenant peu à peu

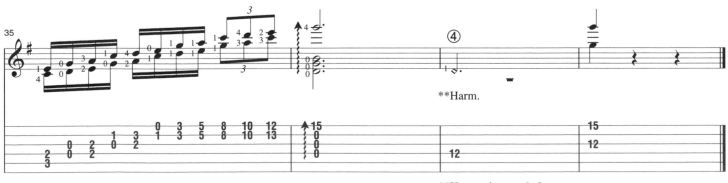

④

**Harm.

**Harmonic sounds *8va*.

Pregunta
(The Question)

By Ernesto Cordero

Tuning:
(low to high) D-A-D-G-B-E

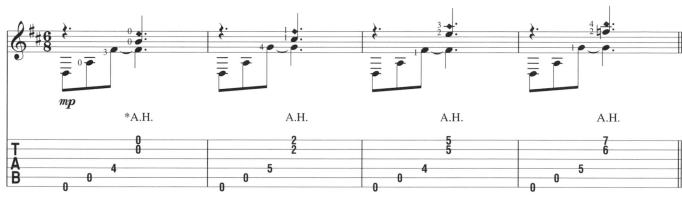

*1st string only, next 4 meas. Artificial harmonics sound *8va* throughout.

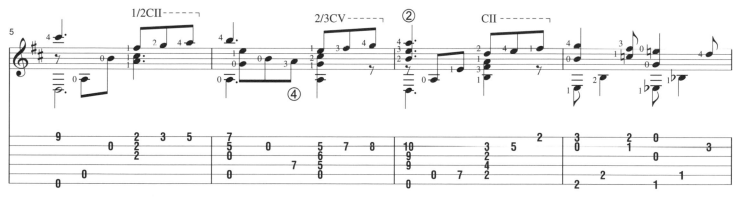

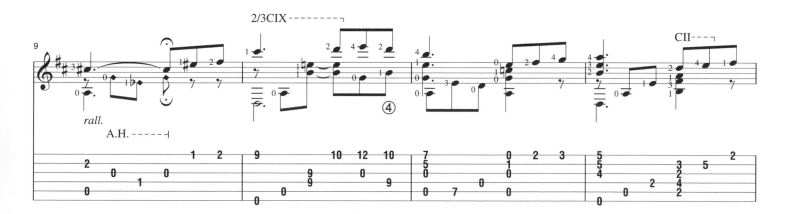

Copyright © 2000 Ernesto Cordero
All Rights Reserved   Used by Permission

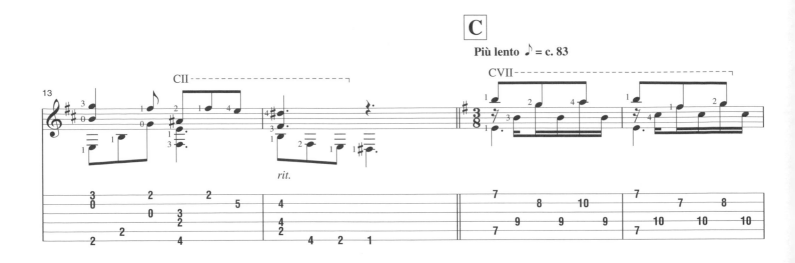

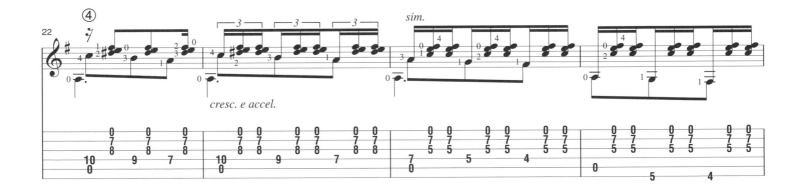

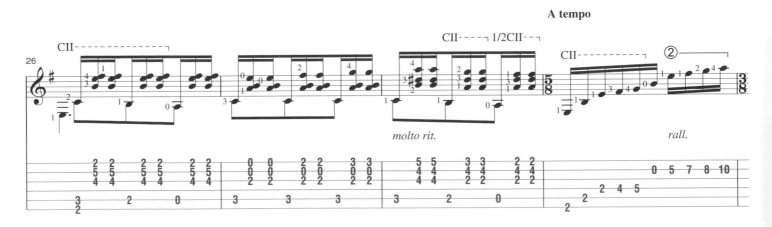

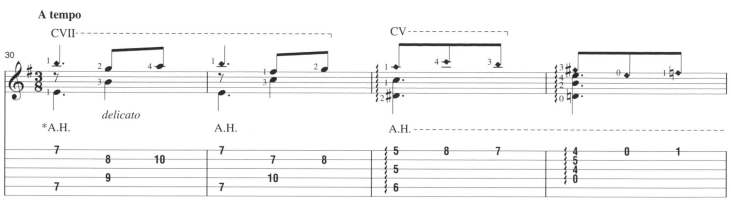

A tempo

*1st string only, next 6 meas.

 D

A tempo

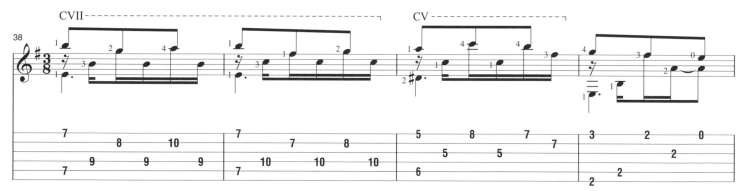

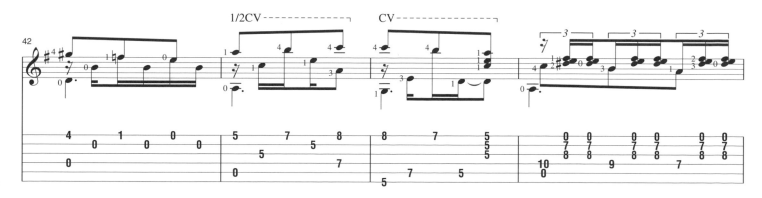

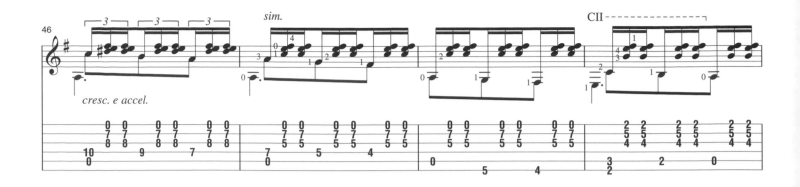

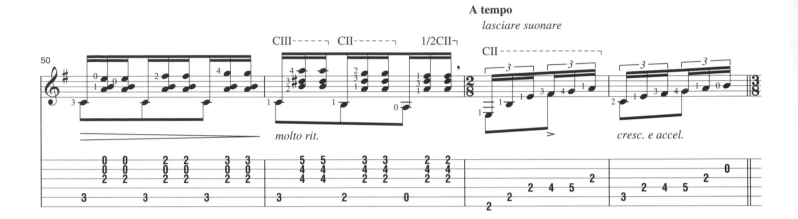

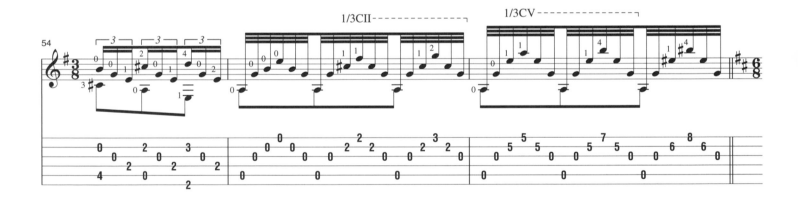

E

Tempo ♩. = c. 48

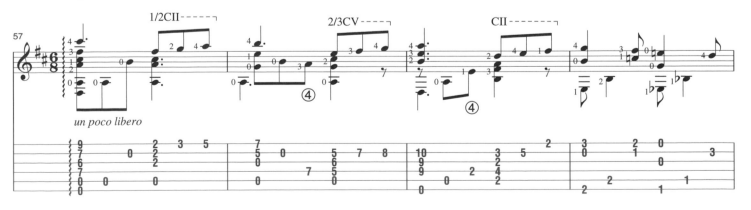

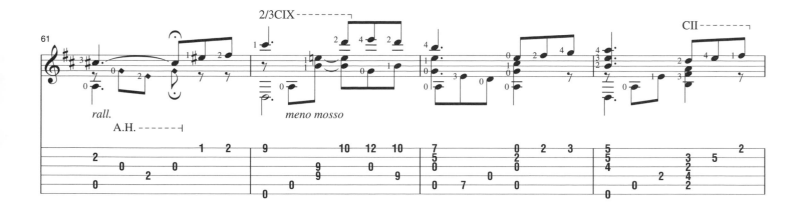

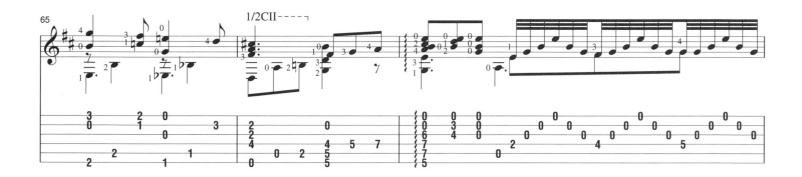

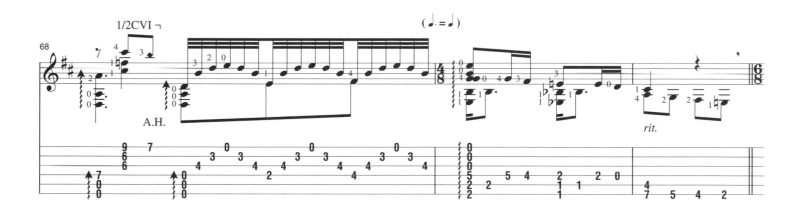

F

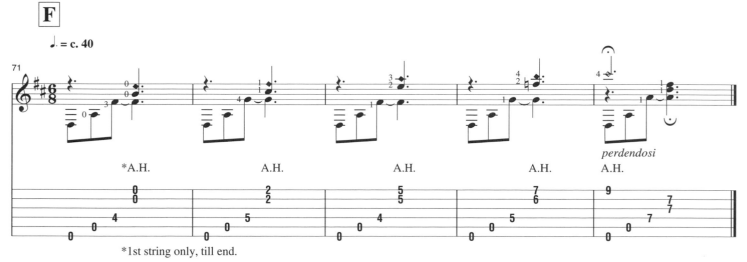

*1st string only, till end.

Von fremden Landern und Menschen
(Of Foreign Lands and Peoples), Op. 15 No. 1

By Robert Schumann
Arranged by Angel Romero

Tuning:
(low to high) D-A-D-G-B-E

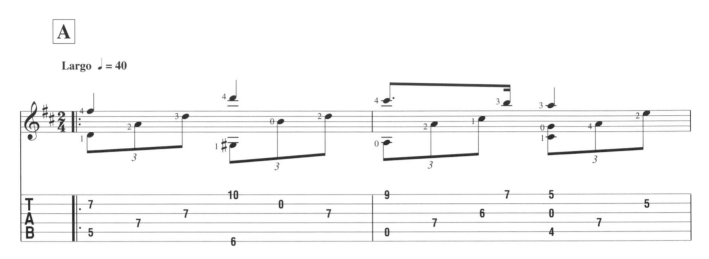

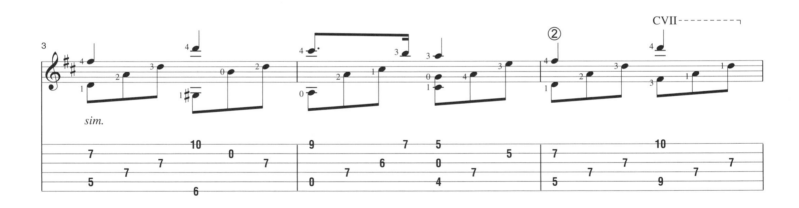

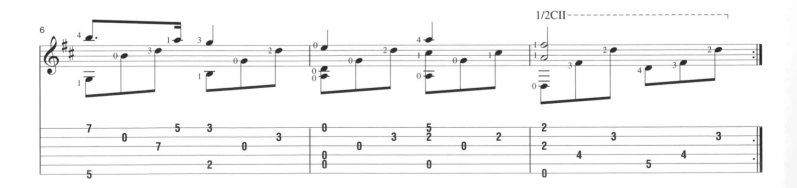

Copyright © 2010 by Angel Romero
All Rights Reserved   Used by Permission

B

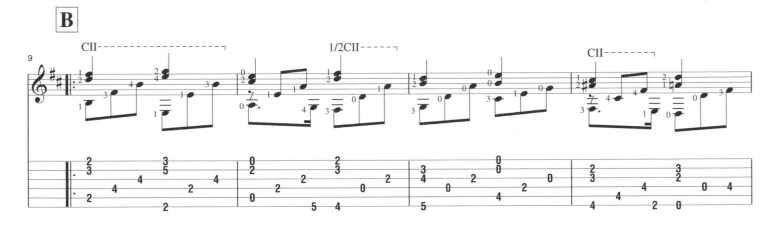

C

A tempo

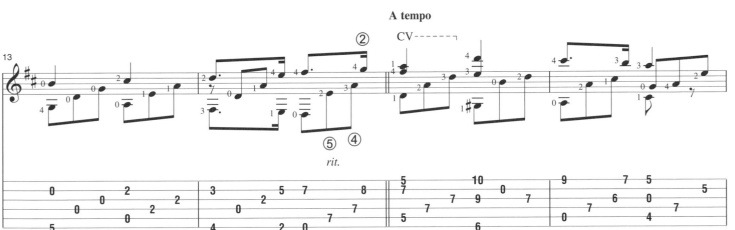

rit.

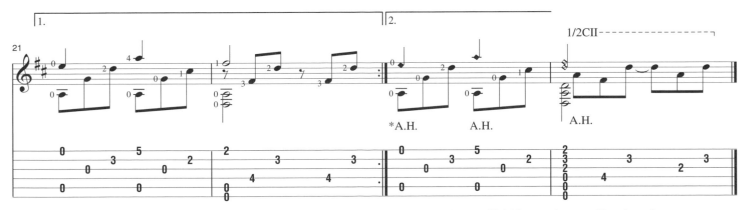

*1st string only. Artificial harmonics sound *8va* throughout.

Träumerei
(Reverie), Op. 15 No. 7

By Robert Schumann
Arranged by Angel Romero

Tuning:
(low to high) D-A-D-G-B-E

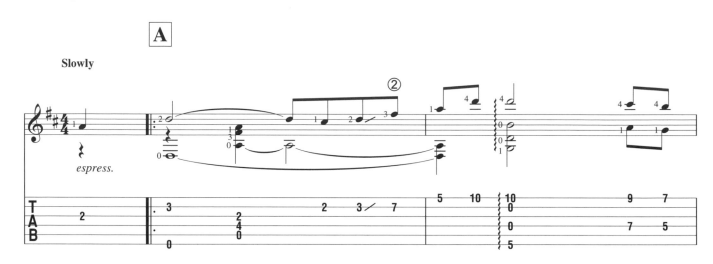

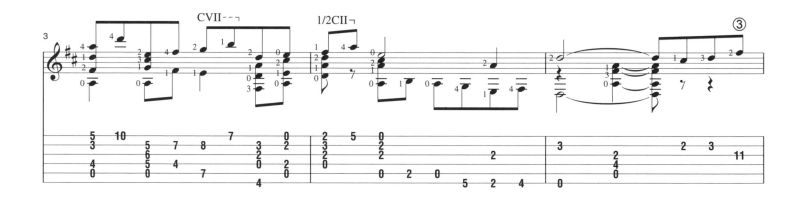

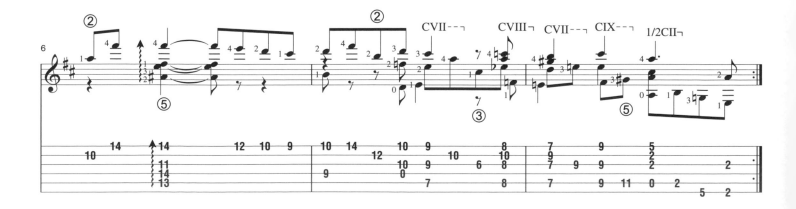

Copyright © 2001 by Angel Romero
All Rights Reserved   Used by Permission

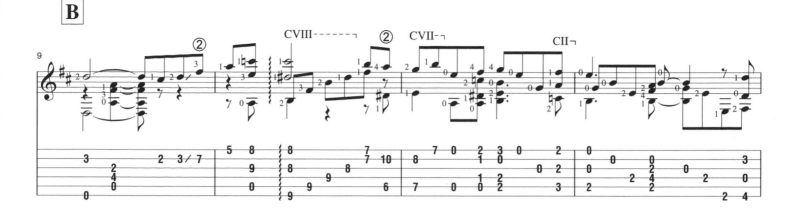

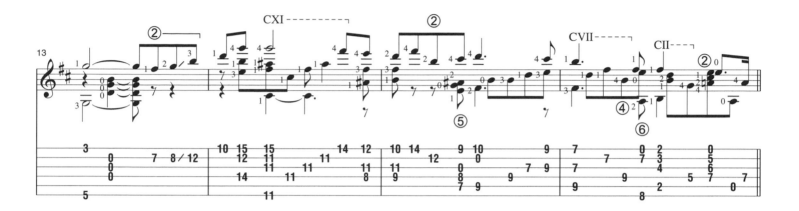

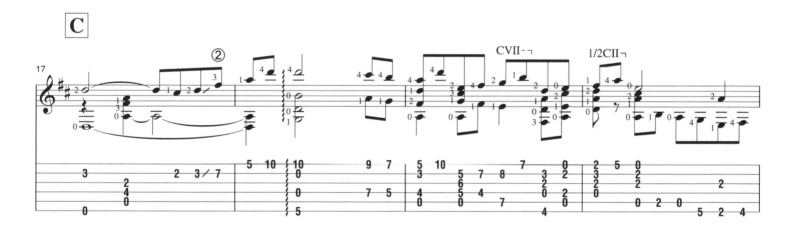

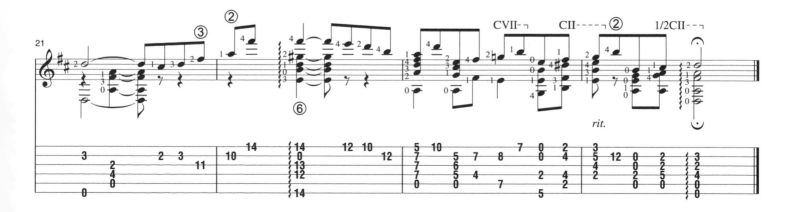

Waltz
Op. 34 No. 2

By Frederic Chopin
Arranged by Angel Romero

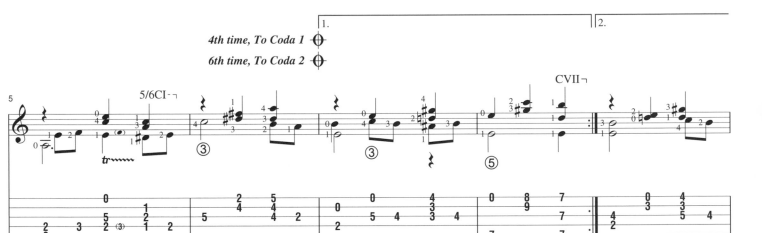

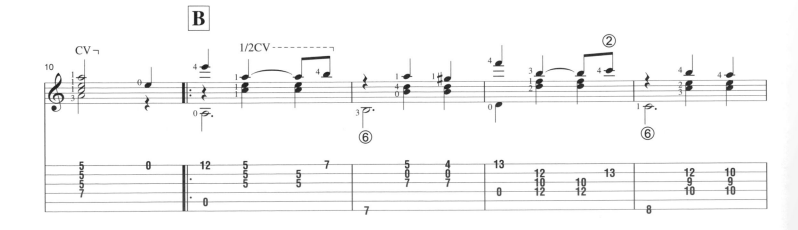

Copyright © 2010 by Angel Romero
All Rights Reserved   Used by Permission

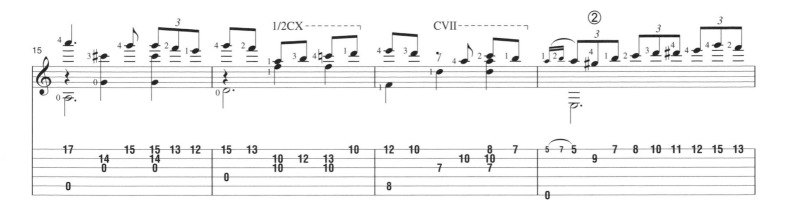

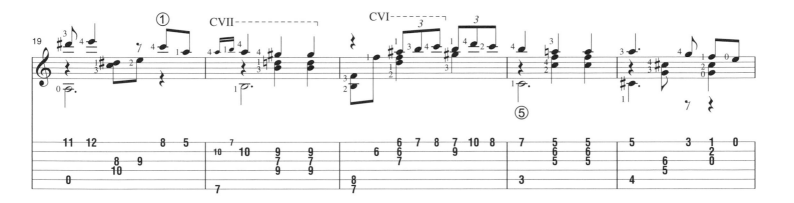

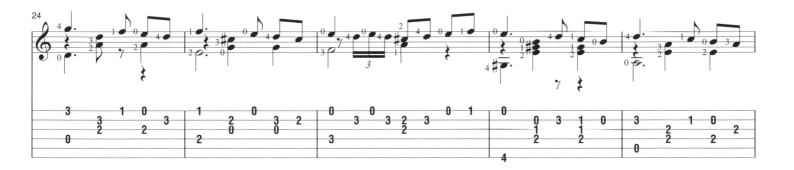

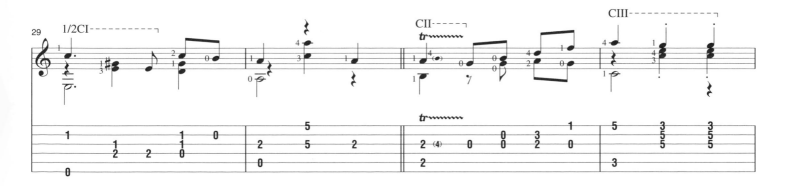

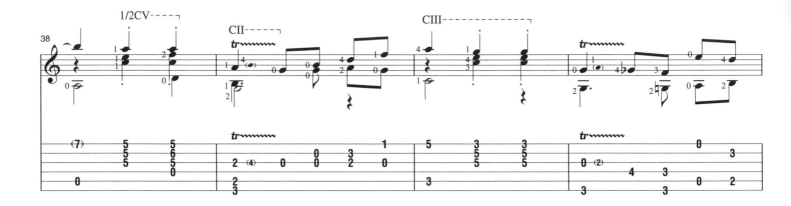

D

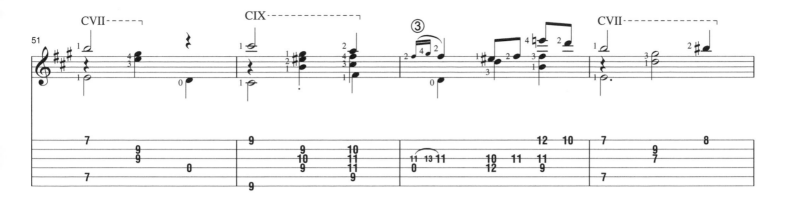

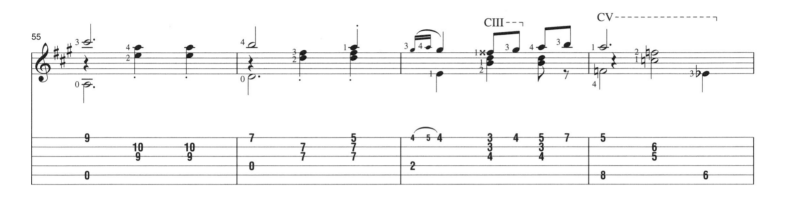

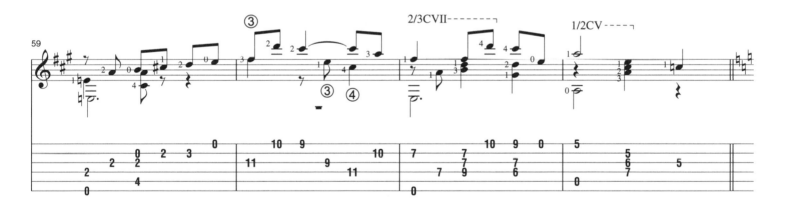

E

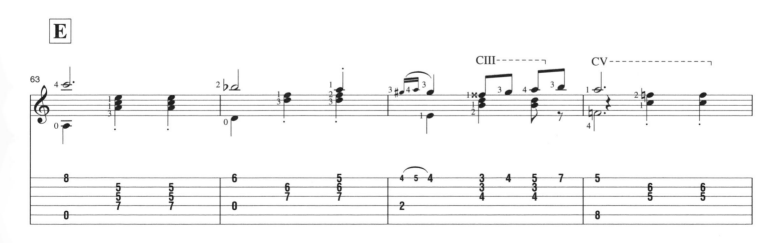

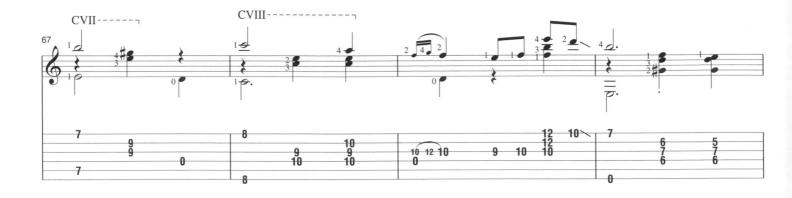

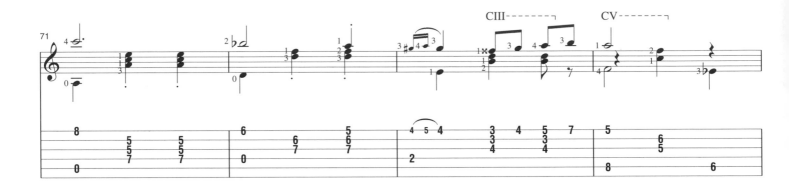

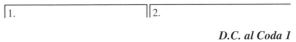

D.C. al Coda 1
(take 1st ending)

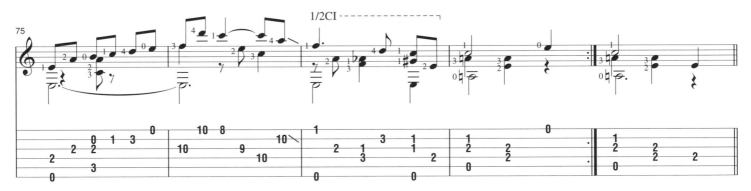

$\oplus$ **Coda 1**

F

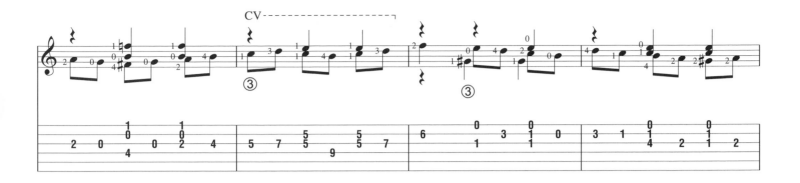

G

D.C. al Coda 2
(take 1st ending)

⊕ **Coda 2**

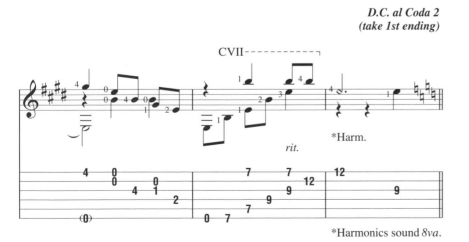

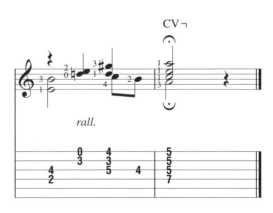

Harm.

rit.

Harmonics sound 8va.

rall.

Nocturne
Op. 9 No. 2

By Frederic Chopin
Arranged by Angel Romero

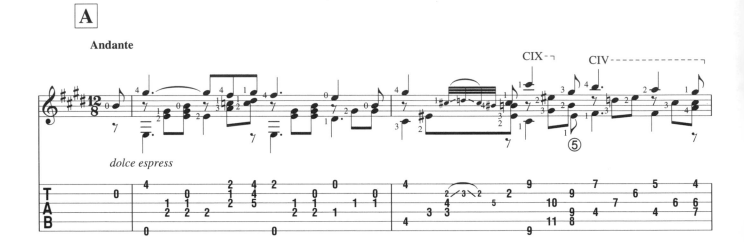

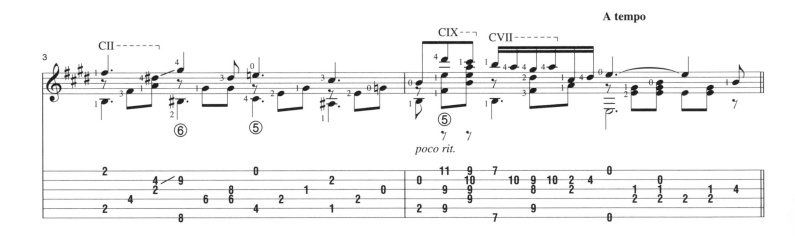

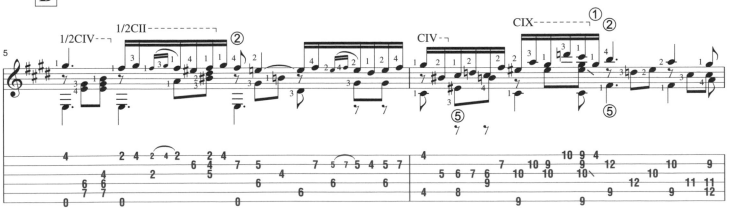

Copyright © 2010 by Angel Romero
All Rights Reserved Used by Permission

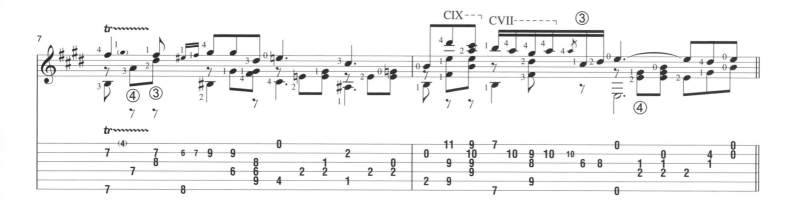

C

D

A tempo

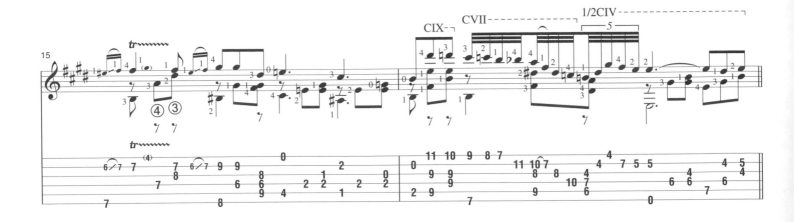

E

F

42

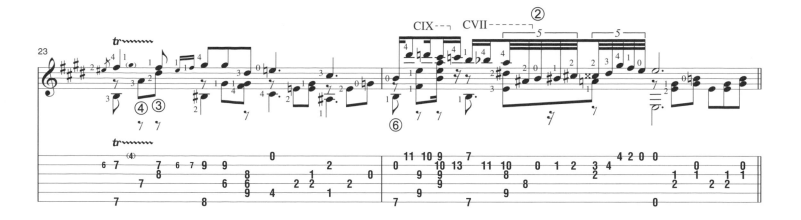

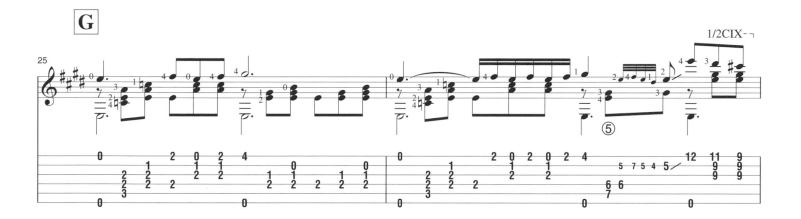

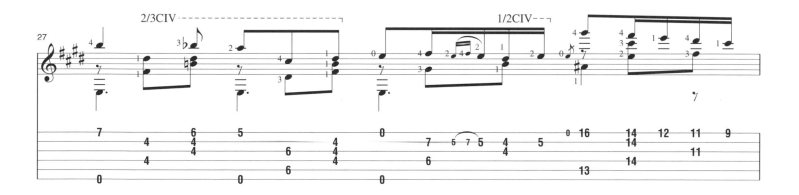

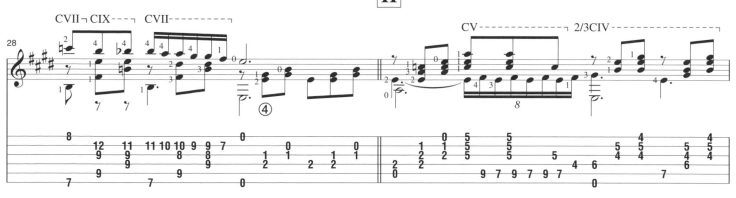

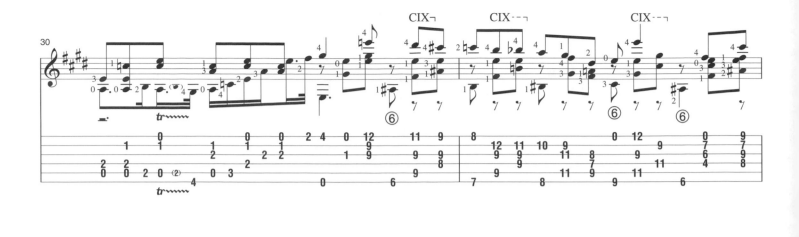

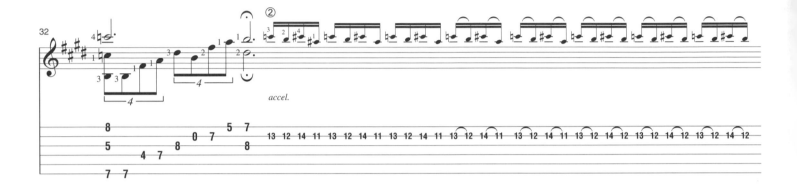

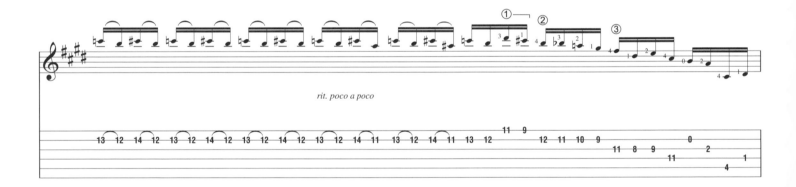

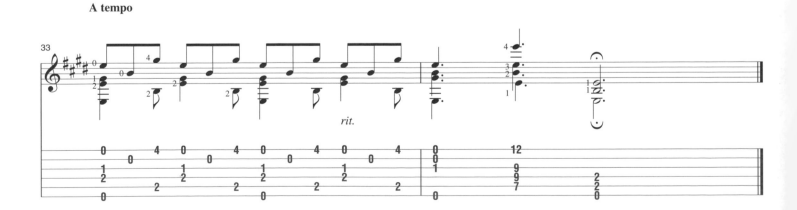

Adagio
from Sonata Op. 27 No. 2 "Moonlight"

By Ludwig van Beethoven
Arranged by Angel Romero

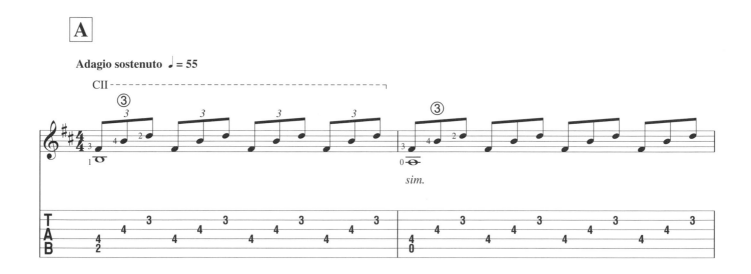

Copyright © 2010 by Angel Romero
All Rights Reserved   Used by Permission

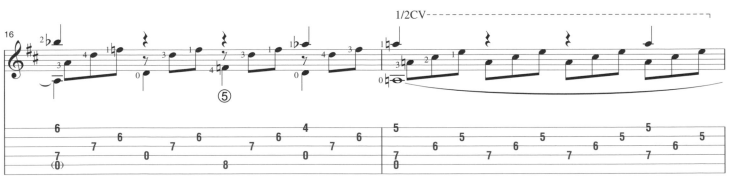

E

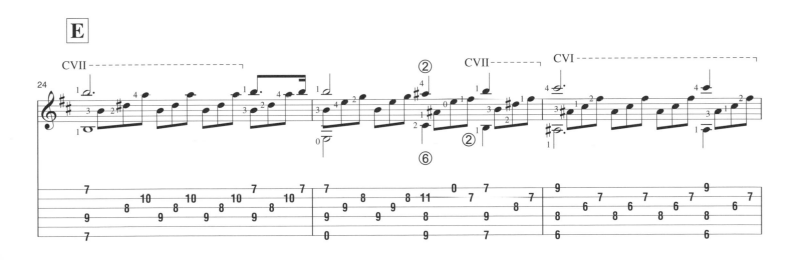

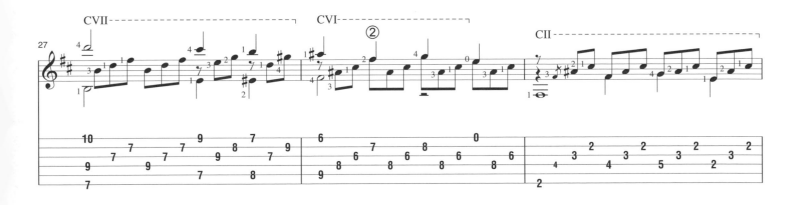

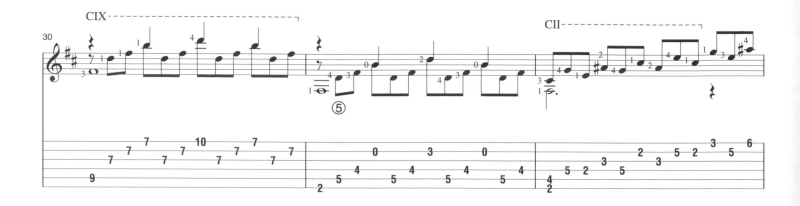

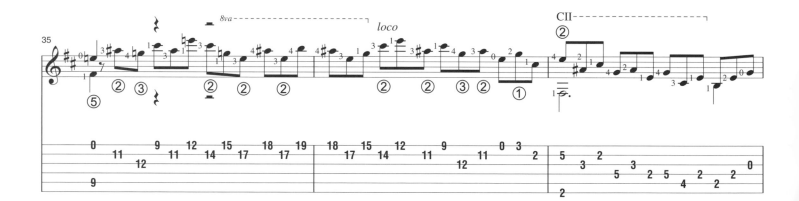

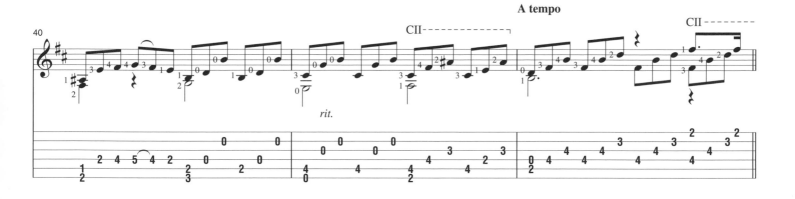

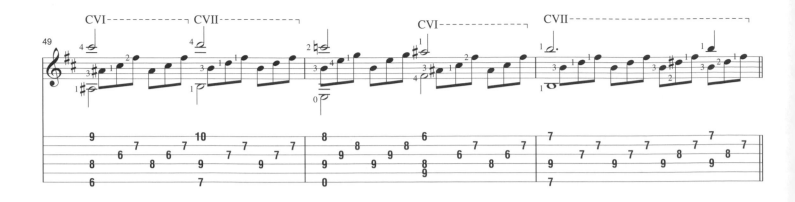

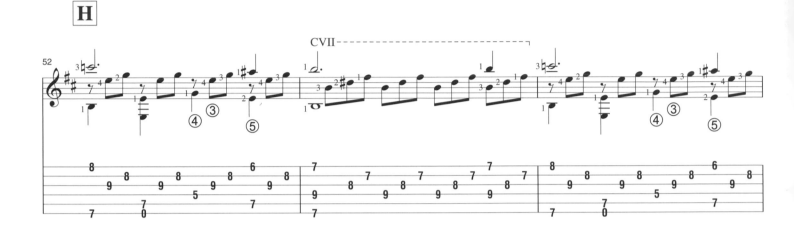

I

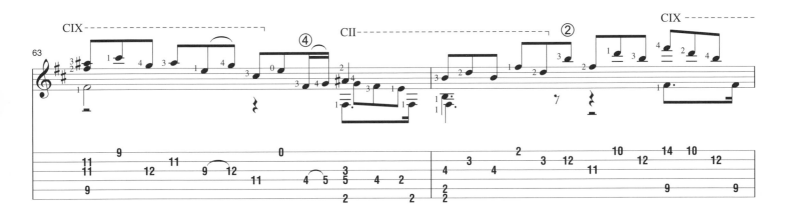

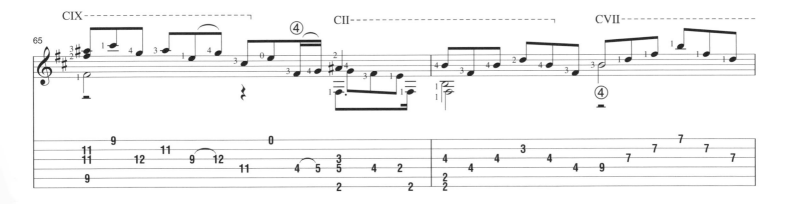

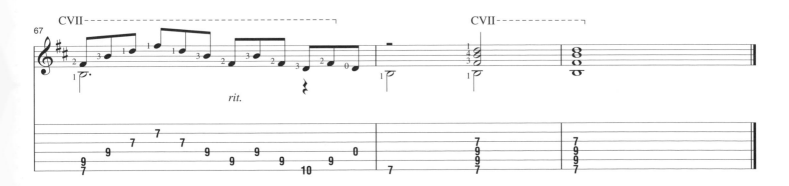

Adagio
from Sonata Op. 13 "Pathétique"

By Ludwig van Beethoven
Arranged by Angel Romero

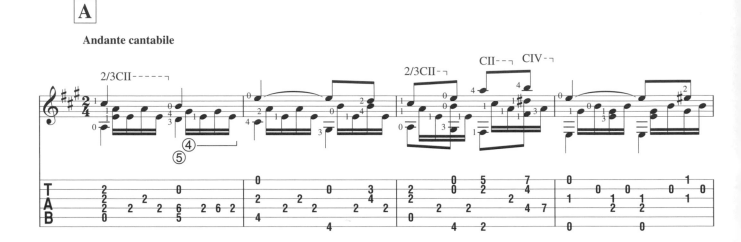

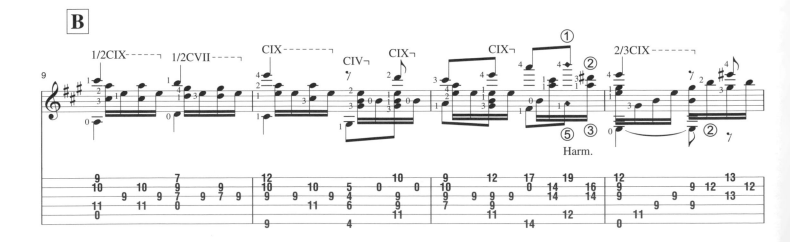

Copyright © 1999 by Angel Romero
All Rights Reserved   Used by Permission

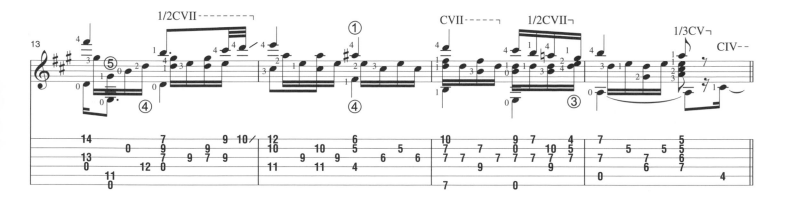

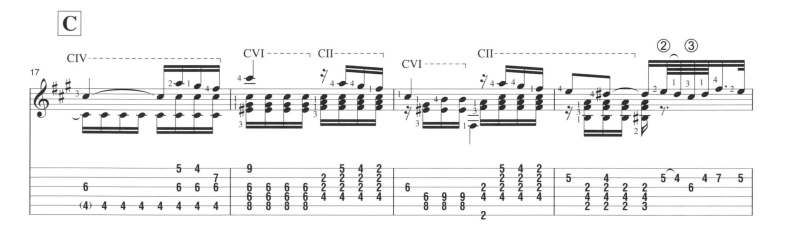

C

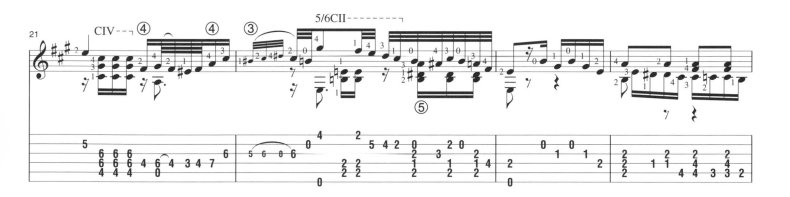

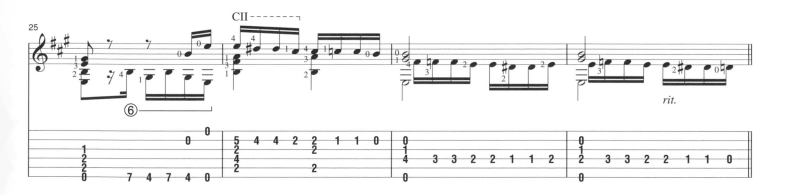

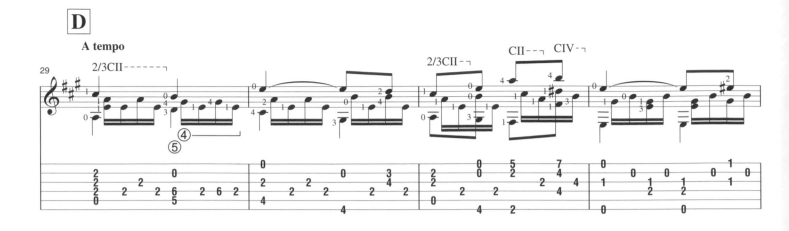

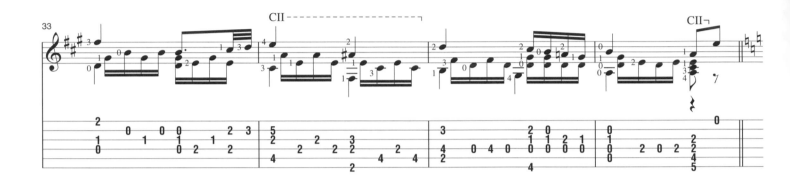

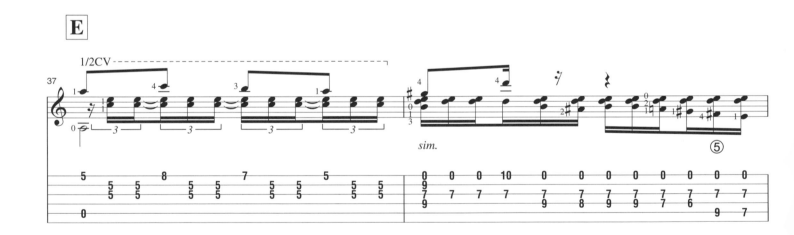

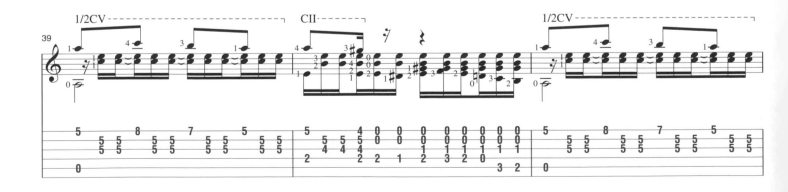

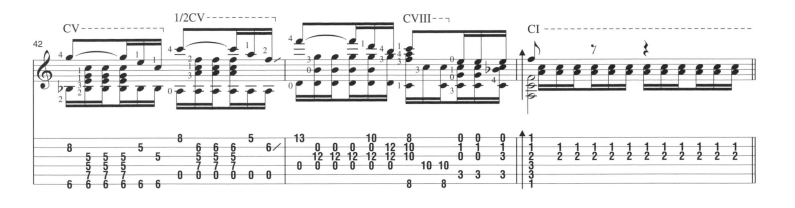

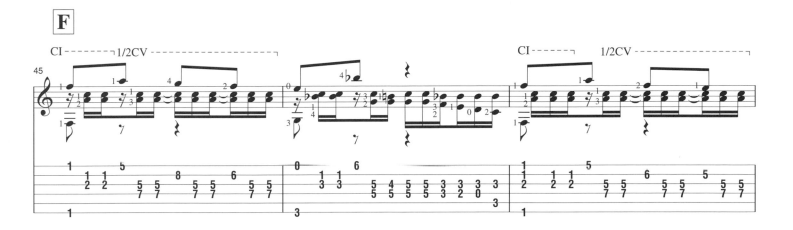

F

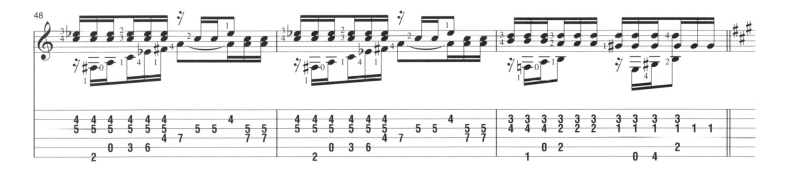

G

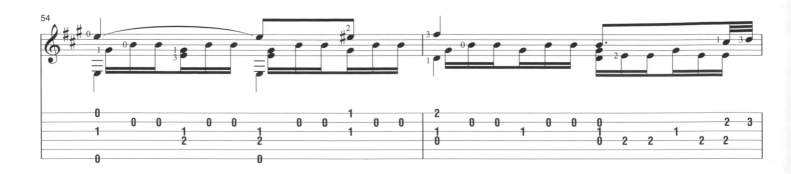

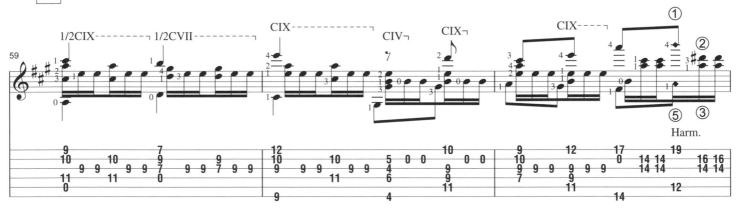

*6th string only.

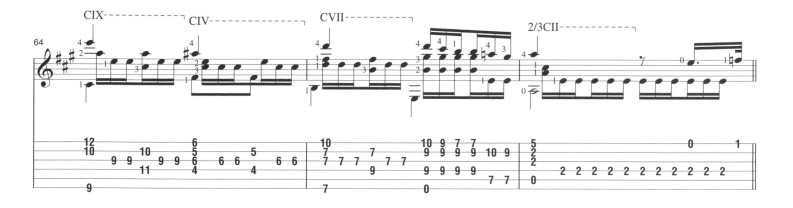

I

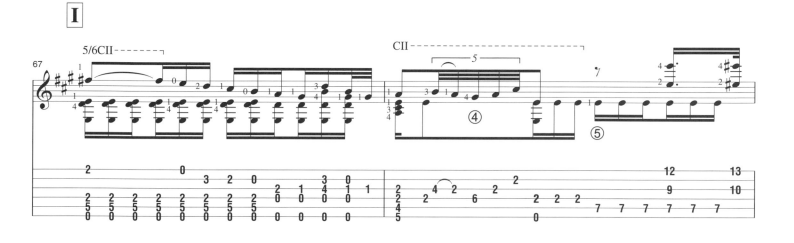

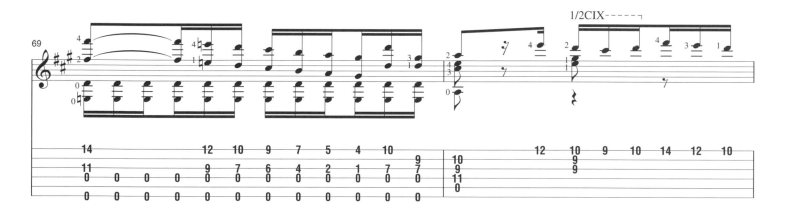

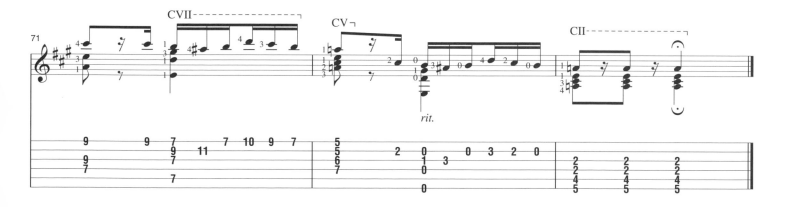

Air on the G String
from Suite No. 3 for Orchestra

By Johann Sebastian Bach
Transcribed by Angel Romero

Tuning:
(low to high) D-A-D-G-B-E

Lento, espressive

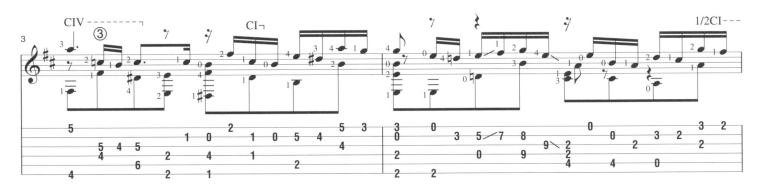

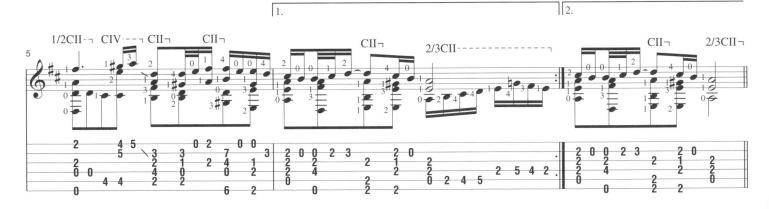

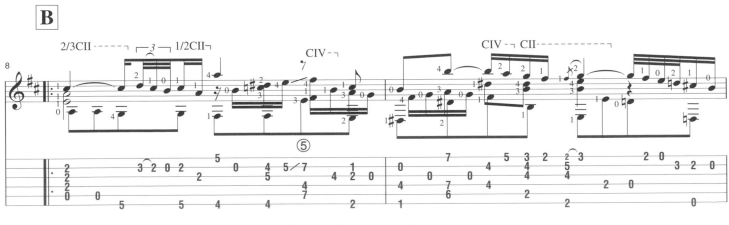

Copyright © 2001 by Angel Romero
All Rights Reserved   Used by Permission

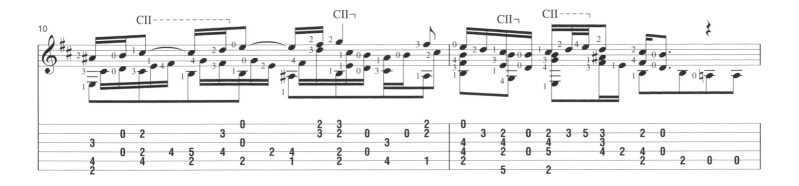

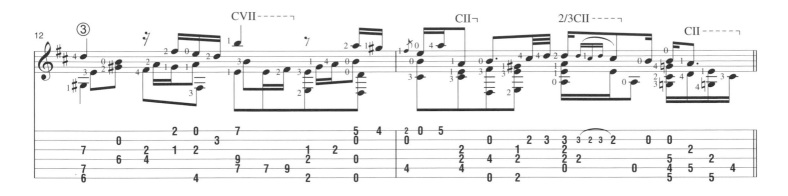

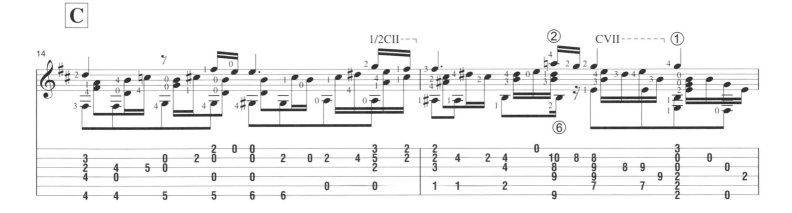

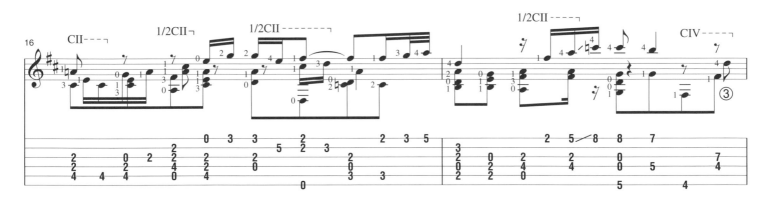

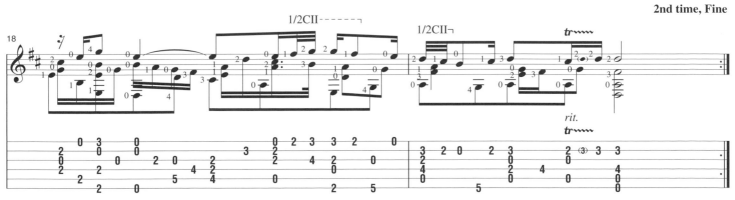

Pavene pour une infante défunte
(Pavane for a Dead Princess)

By Maurice Ravel
Arranged by Angel Romero

A

Dolce, ma sempre sonoramente

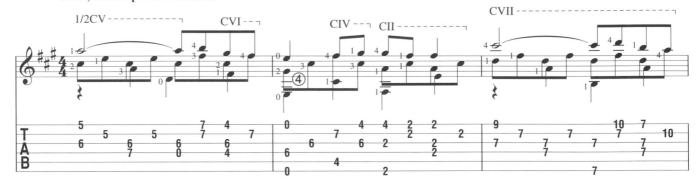

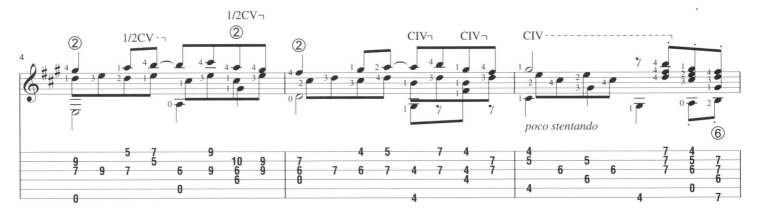

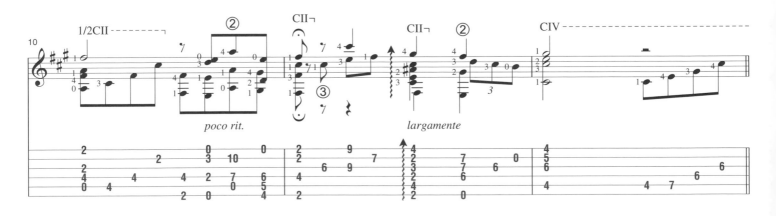

Copyright © 2010 by Angel Romero
All Rights Reserved   Used by Permission

Tempo I *(come da lontano)*

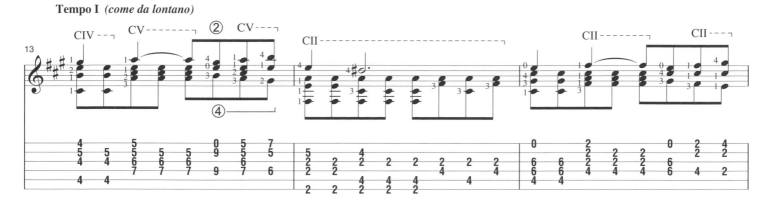

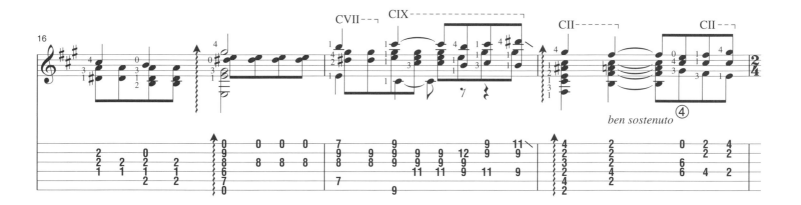

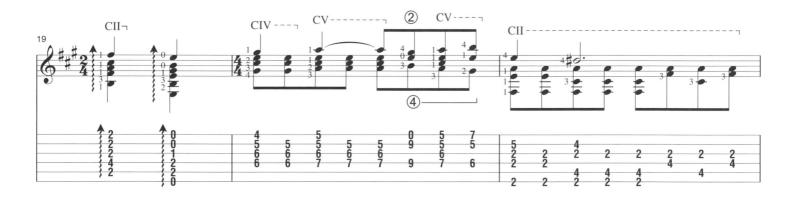

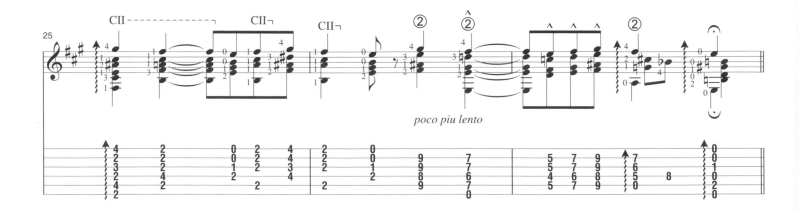

poco piu lento

C

A tempo

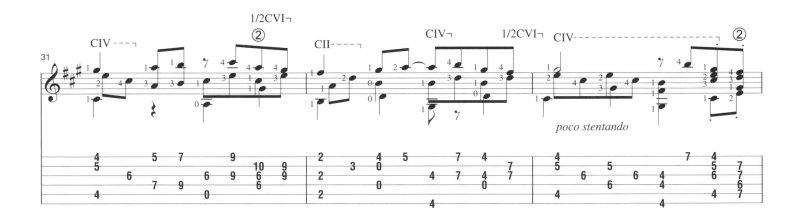

poco stentando

A tempo

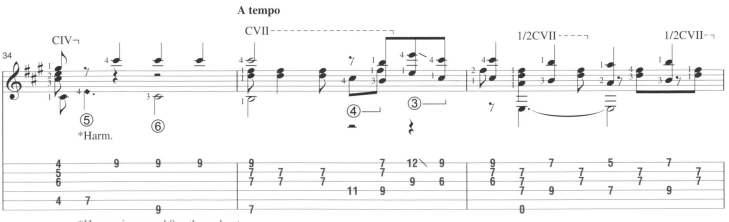

*Harm.

*Harmonics sound *8va* throughout.

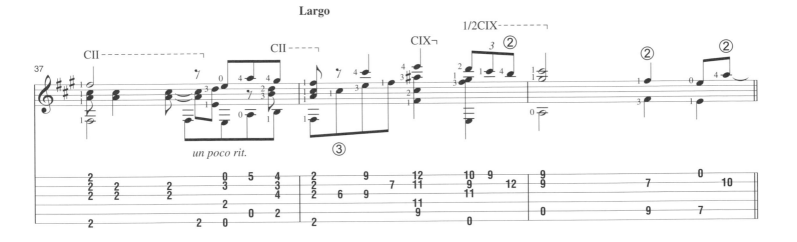

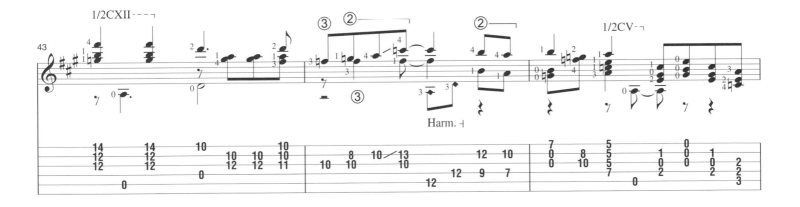

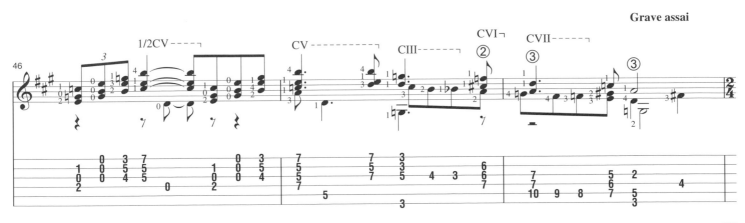

tempo sostenuto

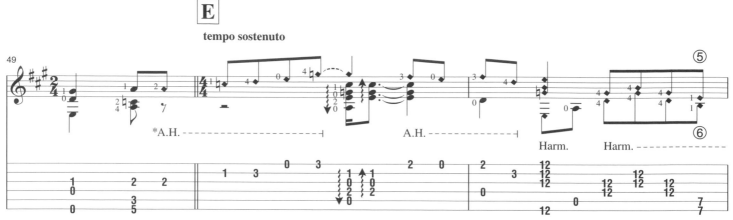

*Artificial harmonics sound *8va* throughout.

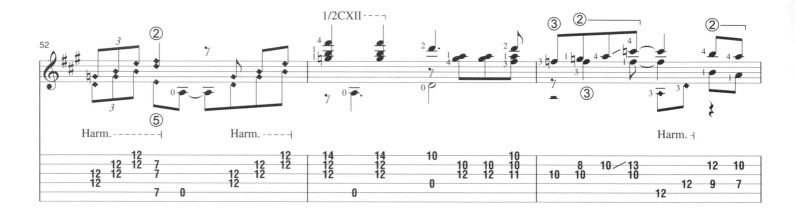

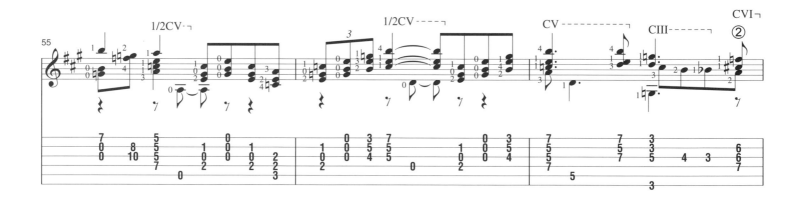

Grave assai

F

Tempo I

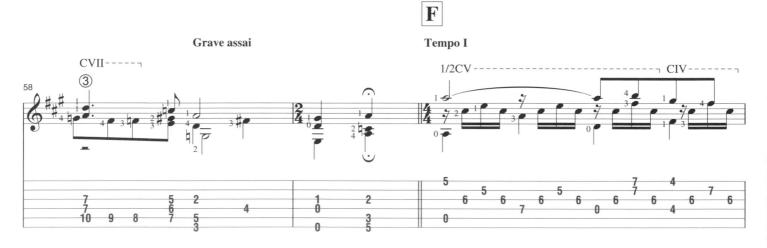

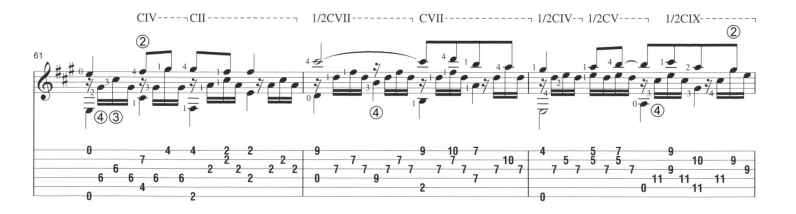

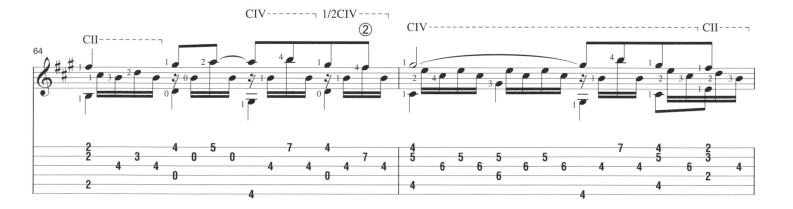

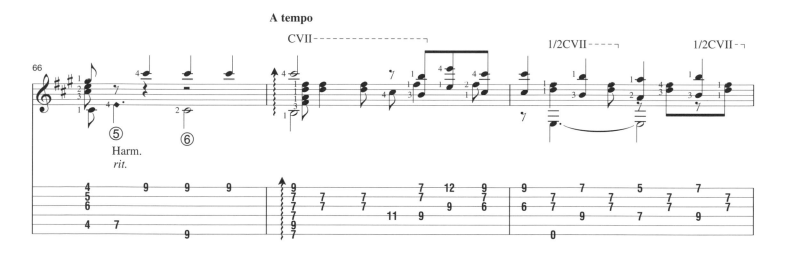

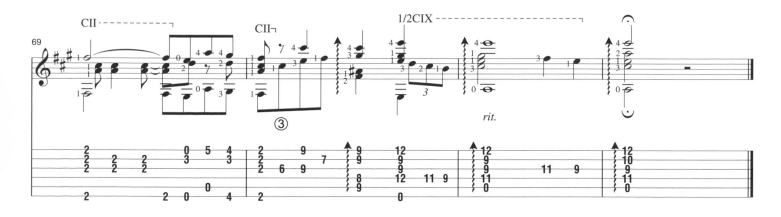

A Prayer

By Charles Crozat Converse
Arranged by Yuquijiro Yocoh
Adapted by Angel Romero

Tuning:
(low to high) D-A-D-G-B-E

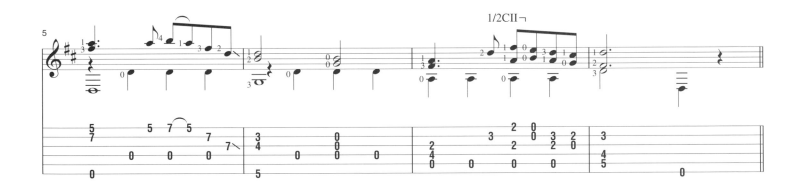

Copyright © 2010 by Angel Romero
All Rights Reserved   Used by Permission

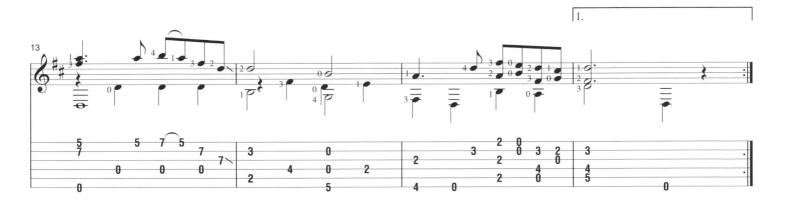

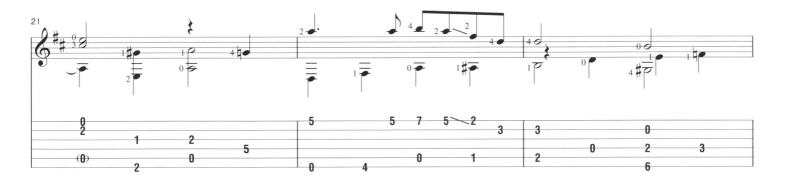

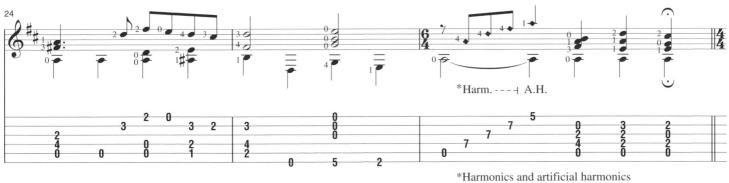

*Harm. ┄┄┤ A.H.

*Harmonics and artificial harmonics
sound *8va* throughout.

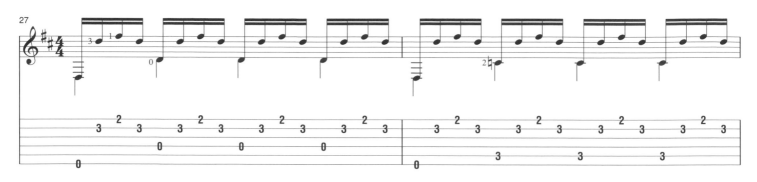

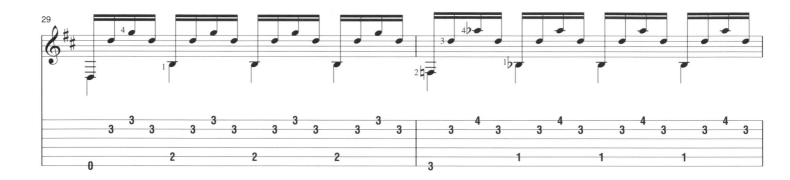

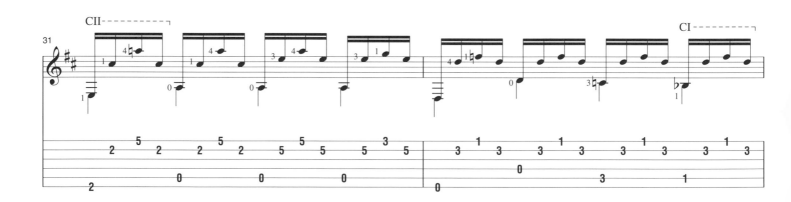

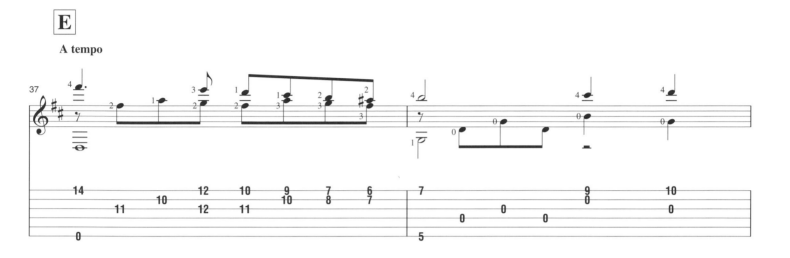

E

A tempo

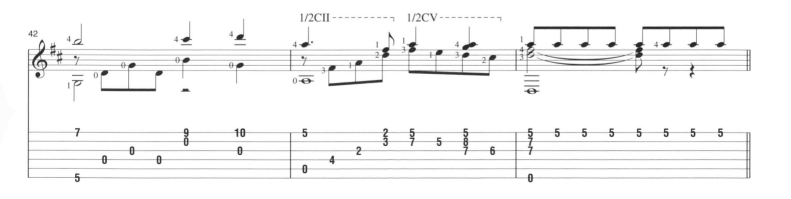

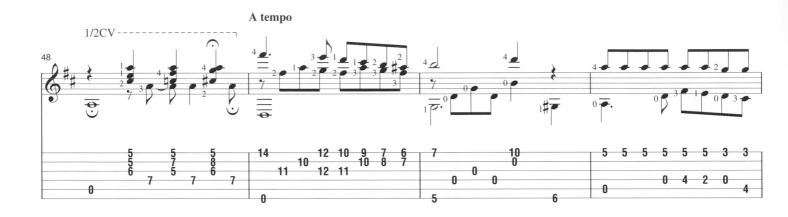

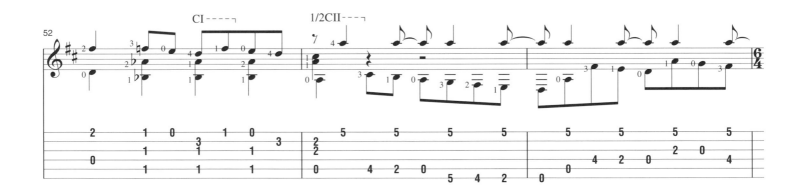

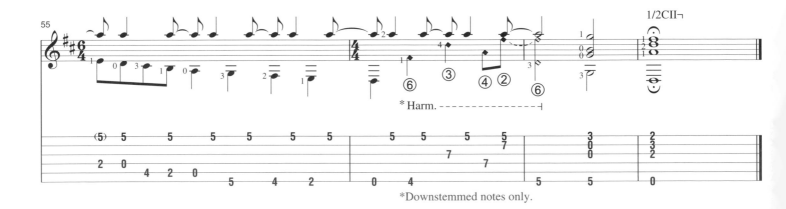

*Downstemmed notes only.

CLASSICAL GUITAR

PUBLICATIONS FROM HAL LEONARD

THE BEATLES FOR CLASSICAL GUITAR

Includes 20 solos from big Beatles hits arranged for classical guitar, complete with left-hand and right-hand fingering. Songs include: All My Loving • And I Love Her • Can't Buy Me Love • Fool on the Hill • From a Window • Hey Jude • If I Fell • Let It Be • Michelle • Norwegian Wood • Obla Di • Ticket to Ride • Yesterday • and more. Features arrangements and an introduction by Joe Washington, as well as his helpful hints on classical technique and detailed notes on how to play each song. The book also covers parts and specifications of the classical guitar, tuning, and Joe's "Strata System" – an easy-reading system applied to chord diagrams.

_____ 00699237 Classical Guitar $19.99

MATTEO CARCASSI – 25 MELODIC AND PROGRESSIVE STUDIES, OP. 60

arr. Paul Henry

One of Carcassi's (1792-1853) most famous collections of classical guitar music – indispensable for the modern guitarist's musical and technical development. Performed by Paul Henry. 49-minute audio accompaniment.

_____ 00696506 Book/CD Pack $17.95

CLASSICAL & FINGERSTYLE GUITAR TECHNIQUES
INCLUDES TAB

by David Oakes • Musicians Institute

This Master Class with MI instructor David Oakes is aimed at any electric or acoustic guitarist who wants a quick, thorough grounding in the essentials of classical and fingerstyle technique. Topics covered include: arpeggios and scales, free stroke and rest stroke, P-i scale technique, three-to-a-string patterns, natural and artificial harmonics, tremolo and rasgueado, and more. The book includes 12 intensive lessons for right and left hand in standard notation & tab, and the CD features 92 solo acoustic tracks.

_____ 00695171 Book/CD Pack $17.99

CLASSICAL GUITAR CHRISTMAS COLLECTION
INCLUDES TAB

Includes classical guitar arrangements in standard notation and tablature for more than two dozen beloved carols: Angels We Have Heard on High • Auld Lang Syne • Ave Maria • Away in a Manger • Canon in D • The First Noel • God Rest Ye Merry, Gentlemen • Hark! the Herald Angels Sing • I Saw Three Ships • Jesu, Joy of Man's Desiring • Joy to the World • O Christmas Tree • O Holy Night • Silent Night • What Child Is This? • and more.

_____ 00699493 Guitar Solo $9.95

CLASSICAL GUITAR WEDDING
INCLUDES TAB

Perfect for players hired to perform for someone's big day, this songbook features 16 classsical wedding favorites arranged for solo guitar in standard notation and tablature. Includes: Air on the G String • Ave Maria • Bridal Chorus • Canon in D • Jesu, Joy of Man's Desiring • Minuet • Sheep May Safely Graze • Wedding March • and more.

_____ 00699563 Solo Guitar with Tab $10.95

CLASSICAL MASTERPIECES FOR GUITAR
INCLUDES TAB

27 works by Bach, Beethoven, Handel, Mendelssohn, Mozart and more transcribed with standard notation and tablature. Now anyone can enjoy classical material regardless of their guitar background. Also features stay-open binding.

_____ 00699312 .... $12.95

CLASSICAL THEMES
INCLUDES TAB

20 beloved classical themes arranged for easy guitar in large-size notes (with the note names in the note heads) and tablature. Includes: Air on the G String (Bach) • Ave Maria (Schubert) • Für Elise (Beethoven) • In the Hall of the Mountain King (Grieg) • Jesu, Joy of Man's Desiring (Bach) • Largo (Handel) • Ode to Joy (Beethoven) • Pomp and Circumstance (Elgar) • and more. Ideal for beginning or vision-impaired players.

_____ 00699272 E-Z Play Guitar $9.95

MASTERWORKS FOR GUITAR
INCLUDES TAB

Over 60 Favorites from Four Centuries
World's Great Classical Music

Dozens of classical masterpieces: Allemande • Bourree • Canon in D • Jesu, Joy of Man's Desiring • Lagrima • Malaguena • Mazurka • Piano Sonata No. 14 in C# Minor (Moonlight) Op. 27 No. 2 First Movement Theme • Ode to Joy • Prelude No. I (Well-Tempered Clavier).

_____ 00699503 .... $16.95

A MODERN APPROACH TO CLASSICAL GUITAR

by Charles Duncan

This multi-volume method was developed to allow students to study the art of classical guitar within a new, more contemporary framework. For private, class or self-instruction. Book One incorporates chord frames and symbols, as well as a recording to assist in tuning and to provide accompaniments for at-home practice. Book One also introduces beginning fingerboard technique and music theory. Book Two and Three build upon the techniques learned in Book One.

_____ 00695114 Book 1 – Book Only $6.99
_____ 00695113 Book 1 – Book/CD Pack $10.99
_____ 00695116 Book 2 – Book Only $6.95
_____ 00695115 Book 2 – Book/CD Pack $10.95
_____ 00699202 Book 3 – Book Only $7.95
_____ 00695117 Book 3 – Book/CD Pack $10.95
_____ 00695119 Composite Book/CD Pack $29.99

ANDRES SEGOVIA – 20 STUDIES FOR GUITAR

Sor/Segovia

20 studies for the classical guitar written by Beethoven's contemporary, Fernando Sor, revised, edited and fingered by the great classical guitarist Andres Segovia. These essential repertoire pieces continue to be used by teachers and students to build solid classical technique. Features a 50-minute demonstration CD.

_____ 00695012 Book/CD Pack $18.95
_____ 00006363 Book Only $7.95

THE FRANCISCO TÁRREGA COLLECTION
INCLUDES TAB

edited and performed by Paul Henry

Considered the father of modern classical guitar, Francisco Tárrega revolutionized guitar technique and composed a wealth of music that will be a cornerstone of classical guitar repertoire for centuries to come. This unique book/CD pack features 14 of his most outstanding pieces in standard notation and tab, edited and performed on CD by virtuoso Paul Henry. Includes: Adelita • Capricho Árabe • Estudio Brillante • Grand Jota • Lágrima • Malagueña • María • Recuerdos de la Alhambra • Tango • and more, plus bios of Tárrega and Henry.

_____ 00698993 Book/CD Pack $19.99

FOR MORE INFORMATION, SEE YOUR LOCAL MUSIC DEALER,
OR WRITE TO:

HAL•LEONARD® CORPORATION

7777 W. BLUEMOUND RD. P.O. BOX 13819 MILWAUKEE, WI 53213

Visit Hal Leonard Online at **www.halleonard.com**

Prices, contents and availability subject to change without notice.

0311